Change In The Wind

Phyllis Reynolds Naylor

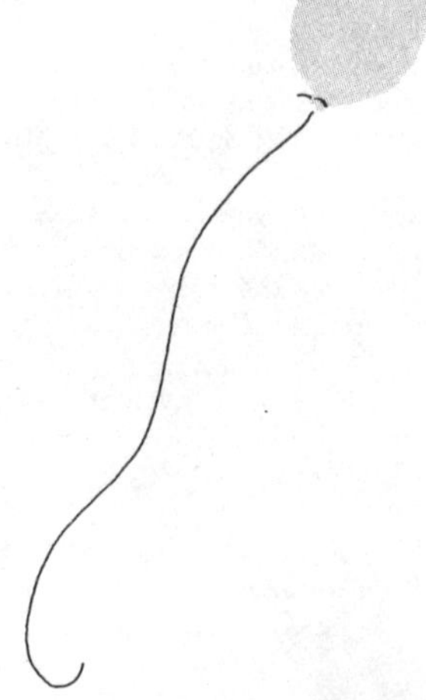

AUGSBURG Publishing House
Minneapolis, Minnesota

*To you
as you were yesterday,
as you are today,
and as you hope to be tomorrow.*

Contents

Preface

Change. It's as sure as the sun tomorrow and the passing of the seasons. It's as far away as the explosion of a star in a distant galaxy, as close as the feelings inside you.

The career you dreamed of at the age of nine may have little to do with what you're thinking about now. The type of person you would most like to curl up with on a rainy night when you're sixteen may be the last person you want to be close to when you're twenty-one.

Neighborhoods are changing, but human needs remain the same. Life-styles undergo drastic upheavals, yet our longing for intimacy, caring, and commitment surfaces again and again. No matter how old or young, conservative or modern, we all need respect, love, and the assurance that beneath the turmoil there are universal truths that we all must discover for ourselves.

Even as things change, we all need a certain stability to function, and a way of coping with the changes that are bound to come. Rebellions and riots may split a country apart, but people's need for order merely takes on a new face. Our bodies change, and sometimes the unexpected accident or illness sends us reeling, yet we grasp what is basic, rearrange our priorities, and put the pieces of our lives back together again.

No one ever promised us that life would be easy. No one ever said that it was fair. But when you consider that, out of 400 million spermatozoa, only one made it, and that one was you, it is truly a miracle that you are alive at all.

It's the only life you've got. For better or worse, it is yours. But the fact that it is yours alone makes it special. You are unique, you are changing, and every day is another chance to live as fully, as wisely, and as joyously as you know how.

The Two Faces of Thanksgiving

Jill watched helplessly while the girl on the bed flailed her arms in a desperate attempt to find the book which had slipped off her lap.

"Don't help me," she told Jill, laughing. "That's the fifteenth thing I've dropped today. I've got to practice retrieving."

"And it's the fourth time you've dropped the book in the last half hour," Jill reminded. "I think we've worked on this assignment long enough. You're getting balmy."

They both laughed. Jill gathered up the notes she had brought along and turned off the recorder. Linda could play the tape later and listen again to the chapter on Theodore Roosevelt that Jill had read.

Linda had found the Braille book and had placed it on the table by her bed. As she put on her coat, Jill watched her. What a pretty girl Linda had been! What a waste. . . .

"Anything particular you want me to help you cram for next time?"

"Only about the first ten chapters in biology," Linda joked. "Thanks for coming, Jill. Tell all the kids hello."

"Sure. Anybody been by lately?"

"Oh, they call up," Linda said, avoiding the question.

"Well, take care. See you Tuesday."

Jill was depressed as she walked home. She was always depressed after seeing Linda. It upset her to think that the girl who used to sit behind her in Spanish had contracted spinal meningitis in her junior year and become a basket case for life.

Then, as always, Jill remembered how lucky it was that Linda was doing so well. The doctor had said she would be a mere vegetable, but he was wrong. Blind and paralyzed from the chest down, Linda still had the use of her brain and her arms—far luckier than most. But how does someone accept the fact of a wheelchair for life? Linda did it by joking. She was always lighthearted. But what did she think when she was alone at night, when the dark thoughts closed in?

Jill opened the front door and was instantly overwhelmed by the aroma of pumpkin and mincemeat.

"Already?" she called to her mother. "Thanksgiving is still two days away!"

"I know, but there's so much to do. I thought I'd get the pies done early this year."

Jill sat down on the kitchen stool. "Know what I'm thankful for, Mom—really, wholly, grateful for? That I'm me, and not Linda Williams."

Mrs. Pollard nodded. "It's a tragic situation, all right —and the only person in the world she's got is her mother."

Usually, by Wednesdays, Jill's other duties and activities had enveloped her, and she was able to forget Linda until it was time to tutor her again. And of course there was Mark. . . .

She'd only known him two months, but she liked what she'd seen, and this Thanksgiving was to be particularly exciting. She and Mark were each to have dinner with their parents, and then Mark was picking her up and driving her to his aunt's home downstate to see the big University game the following day. They'd have dinner out Friday evening and drive back home again on Saturday. Three days with that marvelous guy! Mark was another thing to be grateful for this Thanksgiving, and Jill didn't know how she'd been so lucky.

She hurried home from school Wednesday afternoon, washed her hair, and got out her suitcase. Boots and a fur-lined jacket for the game . . . robe . . . something casual to wear at Mark's aunt's . . . dinner dress and shoes. . . .

Ted, her brother, stopped at the door and watched her pack. "Sure you're not eloping?"

"Not this time," she teased. "You wouldn't miss me anyway."

"Know what I think?" Ted said. "I don't think there's any aunt down there at all. I think that's just a line he's giving you."

Jill laughed. "Mom's already called her long distance. Don't get your hopes up. You're not getting rid of me so soon."

The phone rang, and Jill's father answered downstairs.

"Jill—for you!" he called, and Jill picked up the extension.

It was a voice she didn't recognize. "Hello," the woman said. "This is Mrs. Raymond, the social worker at Central Hospital. We have a rather urgent problem, and I was given your name to call. . . ."

Oh, no! Not Mark! "W— What is it?" Jill stammered.

"I understand you're a friend of Linda Williams."

Oh, thank heaven! "Yes, that's right."

"Linda's mother was admitted to the hospital this afternoon for tests. The doctors think she may have a bleeding ulcer, and they want her here for the next few days. As far as we can determine, Linda's only other relative is her divorced father on the West Coast, and we've been unable to reach him. We wondered if you or perhaps another of Linda's friends could take her for the next few days until her mother is able to leave the hospital. I realize this is a great imposition, for without the special equipment in her home, it takes two people to move her around."

Good grief, what a thing to ask! "Can't you just put Linda in the hospital too till her mother is well?" Jill asked.

"I'm afraid her medical insurance doesn't cover custodial care. They have very limited resources."

"Well, I . . . I'll be away this weekend, so we can't possibly take her here," Jill said.

"I see."

"Listen, I'll call some of the other girls," Jill said quickly.

"I'll appreciate anything you can do. She's waiting

in the hospital lobby. Here is my extension so you can call me back. . . ."

Jill sank down on the chair by the phone. Wouldn't you know it! Just when she was trying to pack, she'd have to spend the next hour on the telephone. Maybe Mother could take care of Linda till she got back. It would only be three days, and. . . . No, she knew that wouldn't work. It would take two people to get her in and out of the bathroom—to dress her, even—and Dad and Ted couldn't help. Mother had never even met her, and Linda would be embarrassed enough as it is without having Jill gone too.

She thought over the other girls in her class and called Charlotte Otis, who also tutored Linda occasionally.

"Charlotte, I've got to ask a great favor."

"What is it?"

"Linda Williams' mother is in the hospital for a few days and they don't have any other relatives here. The social worker called and wondered if one of us could take Linda till her mother gets home. I'm going downstate with Mark tomorrow to stay at his aunt's a few days, and Mother can't take care of her alone. Could you possibly take her? I know it's a lot to ask, but it's pretty desperate. . . ."

"Oh, golly, if it was any other time but *Thanksgiving!*" Charlotte said. "Why, practically every relative we've got is coming. We haven't an inch of space to spare. I just couldn't!"

"Oh—I guess not."

"Why don't you call Pat? Her mother is always bak-

ing cookies and sending them over to Mrs. Williams. I'll bet they'd be glad to."

"Okay, I will. Thanks, Charlotte."

The phone rang seven times before Pat answered. Jill breathlessly told her story.

"For *Thanksgiving!*" Pat said. "What does the social worker think we are? We've all got plans. I mean, if it was any *other* time!"

"I know. I'm going downstate with Mark."

"And I'm giving a fall party for my church group the day after Thanksgiving. I'll be decorating all day. Listen, the hospital isn't going to let Linda just sit there in the lobby. If nobody can take her, they'll figure out something. I mean, there are county centers for people in emergencies. I wouldn't worry about it. . . ."

When Jill hung up, she felt a flash of anger toward Mrs. Raymond. Who did she think she was, imposing like this? A hospital can't just call up neighbors because its patients have problems. Let the Red Cross worry about it. There were receiving stations for homeless people. . . .

The sky was gray outside the window. November was dreary enough without this to worry about. And suddenly she thought of Linda sitting in the hospital lobby, worrying about her mother, wondering who was going to take her and embarrassed about being a burden. Think what a Thanksgiving it would be for her.

No, she wouldn't do it. She simply wouldn't allow her to be sent to a county receiving center on Thanksgiving. Desperately she dialed another number. Connie Blake had gone to Michigan, her brother said. There was one more possibility. Slowly she dialed Marsha Farrel's home and explained the problem.

"Jill!" Marsha said indignantly. "It's *Thanksgiving!* I mean, we're going out for dinner and everything! Pete will be home from college, and Dad's got reservations for us at the Colony Room! I'd do it in a minute if it was any other weekend."

For what seemed a half hour, Jill sat with her knees drawn up, staring out the window. If it was any other weekend . . . ! As though Mrs. Williams had planned it this way.

She thought of how she and the other girls had reacted when they first heard of Linda's illness. They had gone as a group to the Williams' home and told Linda's mother that if there was *anything at all* they could do, *please* let them know. They wanted her to feel that Linda had many friends she could count on.

Linda hadn't really needed the cookies they'd baked for her, the flowers they'd sent, or the records they gave her last Christmas. Linda hadn't really needed friends desperately until this. Where were they now —at Thanksgiving—when every one of them was secretly thankful that they weren't in Linda's position? What kind of two-faced people were they anyway, who helped only when it was convenient?

"Jill, I thought you were packing." Mrs. Pollard came upstairs and looked at her daughter.

"Mother, I'm not going," Jill answered, and she had to force the words out. It actually hurt to say it.

"Not *going?* Why on earth . . . ?"

Jill fought back the tears, determined not to feel

sorry for herself—not when there were girls like Linda who could face life without self-pity.

"No," her mother said when she'd heard the story. "I know I couldn't handle it myself, and I know she'd feel awkward without you here. It's going to be difficult enough as it is. You're being very generous, dear, but I hate to see your plans ruined. . . ."

"Don't make it any harder, Mom," Jill said quickly, getting up and sliding the suitcase back under the bed. "What's one weekend compared to a lifetime? But I wonder what Mark will say."

Her mother came in and gently hung up the dinner dress that Jill had so carefully purchased for the trip. "He'll be disappointed, I'm sure, but you'll have to help him understand. And if he can't, well . . . that's what dating is all about—to find out the big things about each other, the things that really count. I think this will tell him a lot about you."

And I'm not going to tell Linda about the plans that didn't work out, either, Jill promised herself as she went to the guest room to prepare it for Linda. As far as she was able, she was going to make it a Thanksgiving that both she and Linda would long remember.

Love Story, Sort of

You've got to get the picture. Here I am—long hair, wrinkled shirt, dirty jeans, army boots—standing in Walgreen's looking over the heart-shaped boxes of candy. Even the salesclerk thought it was funny.

"Going soft, huh?" she said, smiling. "Your girl?"

"Naw, my grandmother."

"I'll bet."

I paid $5.98 plus tax for a large box and asked her to put it in a sack so people wouldn't stare at me on the bus. Then I clomped out, waded through the snow to the curb, and got on the bus to Tilden Heights.

I just had to do it. Every Christmas since I was twelve, Grandma had sent me a check for five dollars because she'd broken her hip and couldn't get out to shop like she used to. And she always sent a note along with it. This year it said:

Dear Ken,

Don't you dare spend this for socks or under-wear. Buy one of those new kind of shirts that lace down the front, or maybe some guitar music. Have a good Christmas. I'm wishing you lots of snow so you can ski over the holidays.

Love, Grandma

That's why I wanted to go see her. Nobody said I had to. I just knew I should.

The bus rumbled under the railroad bridge and on up the hill past the cemetery. I looked at the gravestones, sticking up through the snow, and wondered what Grandma thought when she looked at them. What did it feel like to be old?

I'll have to admit I didn't come to Grandma's often. It had been several months already. Not that I didn't like her—as a grandmother, she was great. It's just that her age scared me, I guess, like maybe it was contagious or something.

She didn't have much hair left, and what there was hung in white wisps around her face like spider webs. She sometimes drooled as she spoke, and had to keep dabbing at her mouth with a handkerchief. Part of Grandma, in fact, wasn't even her at all. One eye was glass, her teeth were false, there was a hearing aid in her ear and a steel pin in her hip. Sometimes I had the weird feeling that if I reached out and touched her, part of her would come right off in my hands.

I looked down where my own hands lay in my lap and imagined how they'd look all wrinkled. Everybody was getting older all the time—even me. Someday I'd be sitting in a wheelchair and drooling, and I wondered how I'd feel about myself then. I was glad when

19

the bus rounded the hill on King Street and headed for the row houses in Tilden Heights.

I hadn't told her I was coming, but I knew she was there. I could tell by the squeak of her wheelchair when she heard the doorbell. Grandma was always in except on Thursday afternoons when a neighbor took her to the doctor. What was it like to be a prisoner in your own house? The thought depressed me.

The door opened, and there she was, in a lavender housedress, her swollen feet crammed in a pair of gray felt slippers. Her thin lips stretched in a joyous smile, and she flung open the door with such force I was afraid she'd fall out of the chair.

"Ken! You come right in, and don't tell me you can only stay a few minutes!"

She took the words right out of my mouth, so I had to change my story.

"Well, I can stay a little longer than that," I grinned. "How you doing, Grandma?" I bent over and kissed her on the cheek. It smelled of camphorated oil. Then I handed her the sack. "Brought you a Valentine present."

I sat on the sofa and watched while she fumbled excitedly with the paper. The big red heart fell out in her lap and she gasped, beating her gums together. "Ken Larkins!" she said finally. "What did you pay for this?"

"Oh, a couple dollars."

Her good eye fell on the price tag which the salesclerk hadn't removed. I winced.

"Five dollars and ninety-eight cents! You spent your whole Christmas check on me, and then some!" Suddenly she laughed gaily and lifted the lid. "All right, young man, you just take a fistful and eat 'em while you sit here and talk to me."

I obliged, and enjoyed watching Grandma poke around to find one with coconut filling, her favorite.

"How've you been feeling?" I asked again.

She waved my question aside with a fling of her hand. "I've time enough to think about myself," she said. "Tell me about Christmas and skiing and school. And how do you think the President's doing?"

I talked about everything I could think of. I described a stem turn, a snowplow, and a christie. I told her about the college board exams and my term paper and how I was learning to type. I told how the dog knocked over the Christmas tree and about the candlelight service at church and how great the sanctuary looked with poinsettias all over the place.

Grandma caught me looking at my watch and said, "Now that we've absolutely ruined your appetite, you've got to stay for lunch." Without waiting for an answer, she whirled her chair around and headed for the kitchen.

If there was one thing I didn't want to do, it was eat lunch at Grandma's. For one thing, she can't see too well, and her dishes have little pieces of egg and orange pulp sticking to the sides. For another, she saves absolutely everything. When I saw her lifting little dabs of this and that from the refrigerator—a saucer of broccoli, half a pork chop—I knew I just couldn't do it.

"Nope, Grandma," I said. "I've got it all planned.

You set the table and I'll be back in ten minutes with our lunch."

She turned around. "You've brought a sack lunch?"

I laughed. "No, it's special. Put on some plates and I'll be right back."

It wasn't planned at all, but when I reached the street, I remembered the Chinese carryout on the corner. Grandma had never had sweet and sour pork in her life, much less a fried wonton. I spent the remaining money in my wallet, with only bus fare left, and headed back up the street with three small containers in a bag.

"Well, I never!" Grandma exclaimed, spooning some of it onto her plate. "Always did wonder what they ate, and it smells right good, doesn't it?"

The little kitchen seemed to take on a warm glow as we sat there stuffing our faces. I made some hot tea and we laughed at our fortune cookies.

"A full stomach makes better conversation," Grandma's read.

"Wisdom never comes from a big mouth," said mine.

I had planned to stay about twenty minutes. It was now an hour and a half, and I poured us each another cup of tea.

"Such good food!" Grandma exclaimed. "You know what I always wanted to try, Ken?"

"What's that, Grandma?"

She leaned forward and whispered the awful secret. "Pizza—with anchovies!"

We burst out laughing. "Best in the world!" I said.

I helped her wash the dishes and asked if there was anything I could do for her. She asked me to take down some curtains and lift a box off the shelf in the closet. She was glad I'd asked, and so was I.

Finally it was time to go. She was cheerful right up to the last, but didn't ask me to come back. She was afraid it would make me feel obliged. She wanted people to come because they liked to.

I could see her watching me from the window as I went down the hill to the bus stop. When I reached the corner, I leaned against a storefront and thought about Grandma back there in her lavender dress.

What was it about the visit she had enjoyed so much? It wasn't just me. And it wasn't the candy. It was the chance to escape herself, to keep in touch with youth, shake her mind from the confines of her four walls, and be once more a part of the world outside.

It wouldn't be months before I saw her again, I knew. I promised myself that sometime during March I'd be back. I'd bring my guitar and sing the songs I'd heard in the coffeehouse on Saturday nights. I'd tell her about the colleges I'd visited and why I was choosing a Christian college over State. Next time I'd bring Grandma a big flat box without any wrapping on it at all. She'd open it up right there on her lap and find a big pizza with anchovies. And we'd sit around the kitchen, stuffing our faces, talking about how the Italians ate and the books I was reading and how I thought the President was doing.

The Christmas Conspiracy

The reason I was an uncle at the tender age of seventeen was because my sister married at twenty. And the reason I had five-year-old Jason with me on Christmas night was because Elaine and her husband were taking a sort of second honeymoon to Puerto Rico. And the reason we were half frozen to death was because I had taken Jason sledding on the ten-acre tract of land at the end of the road which had been up for sale for six months.

"They're big ice cubes already," Jason said.

"What are?"

"My feet."

"Courage, buddy. Only one more block. Get on the sled if you want, and I'll pull you the rest of the way."

He really couldn't bend in his stiff snow pants, so he just sort of fell on the sled and I went charging down the road while he yelled, "Faster, Eddie! Faster!"

"Good heavens, Edward, he's half frozen," Mother said, putting her hands on Jason's red cheeks. "You shouldn't have kept him out so long."

"He couldn't freeze if you left him out all night," I commented. "Not with all those sweaters you put on him."

We took a hot shower and he played with the drain, damming up the water with his hands and then letting it go in a sudden rush.

"I guess it was right now all the people were saying no," Jason said.

I mean you can't expect to understand Jason the first time he says something. You sort of have to take it apart and analyze it.

I turned off the shower and threw a towel over him. "What people?"

"The people that were saying no to Joseph and Mary and their horse."

"Donkey," I corrected. "Yeah, I guess so. I guess it was sometime Christmas night that they tried to get into the inn, but there wasn't room."

"And so they took their horse to a barn."

No use fighting it. "That's right," I said. I helped Jason into his pajamas.

"Boy, I'll bet they were sorry about it later—all the guys who said no," Jason went on. "I'll bet when they found out it was Jesus they were really sorry! Boy, I wouldn't say no if he came to my house! I'd let him sleep in my bed, too!"

"I suppose most people would if they knew it was really Jesus," I said, trying to maneuver him into bed.

"But what would we do with the horse?" Jason wanted to know. "Put it in the basement?"

"We'll talk about it tomorrow," I promised. I mean, if I lived with that kid twenty-four hours a day, I'd be in Puerto Rico too. Or a straitjacket.

I was fixing myself a sandwich with leftover turkey when the doorbell rang, and Dad welcomed the Simpsons from across the street.

"We were just out visiting around the neighborhood, and thought we'd drop in long enough to say Merry Christmas," the big man said.

"We've got a pot of coffee on. Sit down and have a cup," Dad told them, and I took my sandwich to the family room to eat in privacy.

The conversation drifted down from upstairs, and I didn't pay much attention till I heard Mr. Simpson say, "I hear Mr. Kettler has a buyer for his ten acres up the road."

"Really?" said Mother. "I guess we all knew we couldn't go on having picnics there forever. Who's buying it?"

"That's what bothers me. Someone wants to build a psychiatric hospital for children. Of course, there's not enough room—"

"Depends how big it is, I suppose," Dad mused.

Mr. Simpson cleared his throat. "We'll, there are other considerations too. I mean, the kids would be in and out of doors and up and down the street. We're talking about psychopaths now."

"Has the deal gone through?"

"Not yet. We only heard about it a couple days ago. But the people I've talked to are sure upset."

26

They left a short while later, and I could just see
Simpson going from house to house with his little
piece of news. Somehow I felt angry that he dropped
it on us at Christmas.

"What do you think, John?" Mom was talking to
Dad.

"I don't know. I wonder why it's been kept so quiet?
Suppose they knew the neighborhood would object."

Somehow they left it unfinished. I was waiting for
them to say that they did or didn't care, but they
weren't sure themselves.

I slept until ten the next morning and would have
slept longer if Jason hadn't come in and perched on
my pillow with cereal all over his face.

"Hey, kid, get lost," I said. "Go take another bath
or something."

"What would we do with the horse, Uncle Eddie?"
he insisted.

I rolled over. "Listen, kiddo, it was a donkey, see?"

"Maybe that's why nobody would let 'em in. Maybe they didn't like donkeys."

"No, that wasn't it. They just didn't have room,
that's all. They didn't know it was Christ."

"Then it wasn't their fault!" Jason reasoned. "I
mean, if they knew, they would have let him in, but
since they didn't—"

"Yeah, but it's no good if you only open the door
to the Son of God and close it on everybody else," I
said. "And besides, that's not the way Jesus comes,
see. He doesn't just come down the road on Christmas
night on the back of a donkey with a halo around his
head."

"Why not?" Jason wanted to know, and it was impossible to argue with him.

I got up, shaved, and sent Jason back downstairs to Mom.

It was obvious that the phone had been ringing all morning, because when it rang again, Mother said, "Oh, no! The Simpsons really must have gotten around last night. **Everybody's** upset!"

She lifted the receiver, and I could hear the female voice on the other end, loud and clear. I fixed myself an egg and flipped it dramatically to impress Jason.

"Well, we're not sure," Mother was saying. "I suppose they have to build it somewhere."

"Well, they certainly don't have to build it here!" the voice said. "Why, those psychotic children will be all over the place! People might even think they're **our** kids! It's an insult to the community, that's what."

"Who knows, Eleanor? Some of our kids might need that hospital someday. I mean, none of us is immune to mental illness."

"Oh, Louise, really! We all have our problems, of course, but we're talking about kids who are downright crazy!"

"All the more reason to pity them, I suppose."

"Do you actually mean you'll support the idea?"

"Oh, I don't know. We really haven't decided."

Jason went down into the basement to play with his tricycle and I carried my egg to the dining room and sat down. But somehow I couldn't eat it. I kept thinking about Christ coming in many forms and disguises, and how ready people were to say no. I thought about the desperation of the parents of those psychotic kids, and the conspiracy of good folks up and down the road to keep the hospital out—and at Christmas, yet!

Dad came up from the basement and I heard him talking with Mom in the kitchen.

"Everyone's asking us how we stand," Mother said. "What shall I tell them?"

Dad sighed. "It's an uncomfortable situation, I'll say that. But if the whole neighborhood's against it, I suppose we'll go along. Somebody told me that this is the fourth location the hospital's tried to get, and every time the neighborhood turns it down."

I shoved my plate across the table and went out into the kitchen.

"Morning, Dad," I said, pouring a glass of milk. "Heard any more about the children's hospital? Hope it goes through because I want to get a job as an aide there summers. Would be good experience."

Dad turned around. "As a matter of fact, I doubt it will pass. I mean, everybody seems to be against it."

"You and Mom too?"

"No, but what can two people do?"

"Three," I corrected. "We can at least do as much as the Simpsons. First of all, I'm going to give a short talk about the hospital at youth fellowship Sunday night. And I'm going to start a petition around the neighborhood and see if I can get the other kids to talk it up."

I suppose I sounded real holy and everything, but I didn't mean to. I just didn't want Christ to come plodding in disguised as a children's psychiatric hospital and me to flunk the test, that's all. I just didn't want to be one of the ones who said there wasn't room and shut the door.

"Well, Ed, you've got more nerve than I have, but I'll sign my name at the top of that petition. I suppose the best thing we can do is go see all the folks that Simpson saw last night, and present the other side. What about it, Louise?"

"If Eddie will look after Jason," Mother said. She seemed happy with the decision.

Of course, it took them all day long, and all the time I tried to work on my talk for youth fellowship, Jason was crawling around my desk dropping cracker crumbs in the typewriter. But I couldn't really throttle him, you know, because he sort of started the whole thing. Besides, Christ comes in small ways, even as small as Jason.

The Burden

"Paul, I think Dad wants to come in now. Could you get him?"

On the back porch, Paul put down the sports section and tried to stop the anger that boiled up inside him like a chronic case of indigestion. Not again. It was the fourth interruption. *Paul, take Dad some lemonade. Paul, I think he needs his sunglasses. Paul, turn him around the other way so he can see the Reilly kids playing under the sprinkler.* Dad didn't need him for a companion this summer. He needed a man Friday, a personal servant, a muscle-man who could lift that wheelchair in and out of cars, up the church steps, and all the other places he or Mom decided he should go.

He went across the yard where Dad was sitting, one of his hands placed woodenly on the other. He smiled when he saw Paul coming.

"Want to come in now, Dad?"

"No. I'm fine. It's nice and warm out here."

Paul struggled for control. "Know what? We ought

to strap a walkie-talkie on the arm of your chair so we don't have to walk our legs off."

Dad laughed. "That's not a bad idea. Don't know why we didn't think of it before." He sat for a moment, watching the children frolic next door. "What are you doing now, Paul?"

"Reading the sports section."

"How are the Giants doing?"

"Won four in a row."

"I don't believe it," Mr. Gordon laughed. "Bring the sports page out here and read it to me."

Paul walked back to the screened porch and got the paper. The guilt cropped up inside him and he promised himself for the hundredth time he'd be pleasant. It was only the middle of June. Somehow he had to stand it another three months till school began. College had never looked so good—if only to get away.

Mr. Gordon sat so long in the backyard and required so little else that Paul made a special effort to liven up the dinner hour. He told Dad all the jokes he'd heard in the barbershop the day before, and had him laughing so hard he could hardly swallow his ice cream.

"Hey, Dad, I meant it about getting a walkie-talkie for you. Want to drive to the shopping center with me tomorrow and pick one up?"

"Sure! That'll be great." Dad was delighted he'd been asked to go.

Later, Paul heard his mother talking to his aunt on the phone. "This summer's going to mean so much to him, Helen. I'm so glad we could persuade Paul not to get a job, but to spend the time with his father. Once he gets to college, he'll be so busy. . . ."

The temperature was ninety-four the following afternoon. Paul wheeled his father out to the car. The sun felt like a heat lamp on his back as he bent over the chair and transferred his father's thin, slight body to the front seat, legs dangling awkwardly out the open door. First Paul turned his legs around and placed his feet on the floor, then his arms and shoulders. And all the while his father's face kept its patient, smiling composure which almost made Paul scream with the irony of it.

Here was a man who had been a trucker for nineteen years, whose once-big hands drove the big diesels that rolled heavily across the highways, from one state to another. And then, a year ago—pinned in the cab of his truck when an early morning fog caused a three-truck crash—the big man became paralyzed.

Paul and his dad drove to the shopping center out on the highway where there wasn't a sliver of shade, and the only parking place Paul could find was at the far end of the lot. He parked, got the wheelchair out of the trunk, set it up on the pavement, discovered he was too close to the next car and had to get back in and repark it in order to get Dad out.

He grasped his father under the legs and around his back and slid him out into the wheelchair, one leg, two legs, hands folded in lap. All the while the sweat poured off Paul's forehead and down his back.

It was cool in the department store, and Paul enjoyed the relief.

"I'm cold," said Mr. Gordon. "Do we have to buy it here?"

"Only place I know to get a walkie-talkie," Paul said. Funny about Dad; since he'd been paralyzed, he seemed able to stand any degree of heat, but he was unusually sensitive to cold.

Walkie-talkies were on fourth floor, along with radios and TVs. They had to wait for the service elevator. Once they made their purchase, Paul suggested a soda, but it was too cold in the store for Dad, so Paul wheeled him three blocks away to Woolworth's. By the time they got home again, Paul's back ached and he stretched out on the rug, exhausted.

"It's going to be cool tonight," Mother called from the kitchen. "Cold front coming in. . . ."

"Know what I'd like to do?" Dad said in front of the TV set. "Go see *Gone with the Wind*. It's playing again at a drive-in."

"Good heavens, is that still around?" asked Mother. "Why, remember when we saw that together—years ago! Wouldn't it be fun to see it again? How about it, Paul?"

The phone was ringing and Paul was glad. It would give him time to think up an excuse. Too bad Mother couldn't drive. He picked up the receiver.

"Paul? This is Charlene. Guess who's in town. Ed Peterson—just for tonight. A bunch of us are getting together at my place before we're completely scattered. The last roundup and all that sort of thing. Come on over, won't you? Nine o'clock, and maybe we'll wind up at the falls for a swim. . . ."

"Would be great, Char! Ed Peterson! Gee, it's been months. Let me talk to Mom. . . ."

"Best picture I ever saw," Mr. Gordon was saying. "Always wished I could see it again. Wouldn't that make a great evening?"

Paul's heart began to thump a little harder.

"Uh . . . how about going tomorrow night, Dad? Ed Peterson's in town and all the kids are getting together. . . ."

"Movie's only here for one night," Mr. Gordon said. "But I don't have to see it. . . ."

"Oh, Paul, he's always wanted to see that movie again," Mother said. "It'd be great for him. And we wouldn't even have to take him out of the car."

Paul stopped in dismay, but his father instantly caught it. "Oh, go on, Paul. Maybe they'll bring it back again. . . ." The older man couldn't conceal the disappointment in his face.

"Couldn't you work them both in somehow, darling?" Mrs. Gordon said. "It would mean *so* much to Dad. . . ."

It was no use. Even if Paul went to the party, he couldn't enjoy it. How long was that movie anyway— four hours?

"Char, I just can't," Paul said, moving the receiver into the hallway again. "Dad's got his heart set on *Gone with the Wind*. I wish I could, I really do. . . ."

The movie lasted four hours, but it seemed eight —an eternity of syrup and sentiment to Paul that left him absolutely flat. He tried to think of something positive to say about it on the way home, but he couldn't.

The back porch was cool, and Paul had a bed there next to Dad's. As Paul placed his father on his back, Mr. Gordon said, "Why don't you give Charlene a call and see if the party's still going on?"

"Maybe I will," said Paul. He phoned.

"Oh, I'm sorry, Paul," Charlene said. "Ed had to catch an early plane, so we broke up early. The last couple just left. Ed said he was real sorry to miss you. It was really great. Everybody was here. . . ."

Paul took off one shoe and let it thump heavily on the floor beside his bed. His one opportunity to see everybody. The last summer, probably, that they'd all be together. Fury boiled up inside him. All the way home Mom and Dad had talked about Paul's taking his father to a high school reunion, so he could show his son off to all the old guys he hadn't seen in years. Was it going to be like this all summer? Was Paul to sacrifice everything he wanted to do just to please Dad? He took off the other shoe and threw it down.

"Can't you get the fly swatter and look for that mosquito?" Mr. Gordon asked.

"All right! All right! Just give me a chance, will you?" Paul stopped, furious—too furious to think. "I'm sorry," he said, but his voice was harsh. "Tired, I guess."

There was silence from the other bed. Finally his father said, "I guess you're pretty disappointed about the party."

"Yeah. I guess so. My only chance to see everybody, and I've gotta play the man-servant bit."

"Go ahead, Paul. Get it off your chest."

"I've said too much."

"No. Not enough. Go on. . . ."

Paul wheeled about suddenly. "Look, let me alone, will you? I'm with you twenty-four hours a day. Do you have to creep inside my head too?"

He yanked at the light chain and flopped back on the bed, his face hot and his chest heaving in the darkness. Outside the locusts whirred, but the porch was quiet.

Paul put one arm over his eyes. What was the matter with him? Did he want to ruin the summer completely for Dad?

"You may not think so, Paul, but I know exactly how you feel. And I'm glad you told me." His father's voice sounded strangely deep and strong from the other bed. "There was a time in my life when I didn't have half the patience you've had with me, and I complained more bitterly than I've heard you do yet."

The strength in his father's voice seemed to relax Paul. "When?" Paul asked finally. "I never heard about it."

"I know. I got it out of my system before you were born. It was right after your mother and I were married. I had big plans, plans you never knew about, I guess. I wanted to go to college. Nobody had ever been to college in my family before, and I wanted to be a construction engineer on apartment buildings and things. Your mother was going to work and put me through college. I'd only gone two months when we found out she was expecting a baby."

Paul lowered his arm and turned his head in the darkness. "Me?"

"Yep. Not exactly what we planned. It was a hard time for Marie. I was really bitter—horrible to live with."

There was such a prolonged silence that Paul wondered if his father was reliving the experience again.

"They say," Paul ventured finally, "that if you really want to do something, you'll find a way."

"That's what I told myself," his father said. "I could go to school nights—get it in twelve years instead of four. But it seemed as though everything conspired to stop me. My dad died and my brother and I had to keep the farm going for my mother. It was the only income she had. I got a job driving trucks because it was the highest paying job I could find, and when I wasn't on the road, I was on the farm helping out. There was no time for school then, so I finally gave up the dream. But not without protest. . . ."

"I . . . never even guessed," Paul said finally.

"I know. I decided I had to adjust to what life had given me, or lose everything I had—Marie, you, and my own self-respect. I chose the first, but it wasn't easy."

"And then the accident you had no control over, on a job you never wanted. . . ."

"The final irony, isn't it? I've thought about it many times. But things could have been worse. I still have my mind; at least that wasn't injured. I'm not about to throw that away too because I can't have all the trimmings."

The silence this time settled over the back porch like a summer blanket. His father's confession had so stunned Paul that he felt he was unable to cope with it at first. Gradually, as his mind sorted out the details, the feelings began to come through again and Paul explored them one by one.

What was it he felt now? Guilt? No. He felt no responsibility for what had happened to his father. Grief? Some, but not overwhelming. He had lived through that the month after the accident when he had felt his father's sadness in all its intensity.

Instead he felt a strange kind of empathy, an awareness of his father as he'd never felt it before, and a concern for his father's needs that somehow dwarfed his own need for one great last summer. What was a summer compared to a whole lifetime ahead of him? Relatively nothing. What was one summer to Dad, when most of his summers were behind him? Everything.

"Dad," he said. "You were talking about that high school reunion of yours. . . . I want you to go, and I want to go with you. I'd be . . . proud."

"So would I, Paul," said Mr. Gordon. "Yes—if you think you'd enjoy it, I'd like to go."

How It Was
with Mom

The thing Jackie remembered most about Mother's Day was the awful squabble she and her mother had the previous evening, clouding that Sunday with memories of the night before. It was all because Jackie had dated Clyde Martin five Saturdays in a row.

"What difference does it make?" Jackie had snapped, brushing her long hair till it glistened around her shoulders. "You always let me date on Saturday nights as long as I'm in by eleven-thirty."

Mother chose her words carefully. "It's just that Clyde's . . . not your type, Jackie, and I think you know it. He's not someone I'd want you to get serious about."

"So who's getting serious?" Jackie asked in exasperation.

"Well, when you date him week after week, what am I supposed to think?"

"Good grief, Mom, five dates isn't a lifetime! He's lots of fun, but that's all there is to it."

But Mrs. Cleaver brought up the subject of going

along with the crowd, and Jackie brought up the subject of trust, and from there it degenerated into accusations of immaturity on one side and stodginess on the other, so that when Clyde knocked at eight, Mrs. Cleaver retired to the kitchen in hurt silence and Jackie sailed angrily out the door to the waiting car.

It all came back clearly now as Jackie fried the eggs at breakfast. And later, as she wrestled with the automatic washer, listening for the front door and Gretchen's voice, she wondered if she and her mother ever would bridge the gap between them.

Mother's emergency operation had happened so suddenly that there was no time to make arrangements with relatives. All Jackie remembered was her mother's illness one night at dinner, and when she woke the next morning, there was a note saying that Mom had gone to the hospital during the night.

It was all over now. Mom would be home in a week, and all Jackie had to do meanwhile was the housework, the cooking, and the laundry, not to mention keeping an eye on thirteen-year-old Gretchen. That, she decided, was the hardest of all.

She went upstairs with a basket of sheets and started lunch. But the tomato soup was cold and the sandwiches stale when Gretchen flipped in an hour and a half later with an ice cream bar, sprawling on the couch to eat it.

"For heaven's sake, Gretchen, you haven't even had lunch yet!" Jackie snapped, marching into the living room. "Where in the world have you been?"

Gretchen stared at her as one observes a frenzied

colony of ants and went on eating the ice cream. "At the drugstore! I *told* you I was going there!"

"Gretchen, that was two hours ago! How long does it take to buy a notebook and some hair clips?"

"Well, I had to wait for Sally to get dressed, and we stopped at her cousin's. And Leeds' didn't have the right size notebook, so we had to try Murphy's, and. . . ."

"Then why didn't you *call* me? What am I supposed to think when I expect you home in fifteen minutes and you're gone for two hours?"

Gretchen looked at her wide-eyed. "But you didn't *say* to come straight home."

Jackie's shoulders sagged. "Come on out in the kitchen and eat what's left of lunch," she said tersely. "And don't you dare get chocolate on that couch."

There was no time for a date with Clyde this Saturday night. Dad had to have a clean shirt for church the next day, and there were groceries to buy, homework to be done, and another visit to the hospital at eight.

Mother was feeling better, and the color was back in her cheeks.

"How are you managing, honey?" she asked Jackie. "It must be hard."

"Well, things seem to get done, but not the way you'd do them," Jackie said cheerfully. "The biggest problem is—" She started to say Gretchen, but stopped. No use worrying her mother about that. "I'm not sure I'm ironing Dad's shirts the way he likes them."

"Don't worry about me," Dad said good-naturedly. "Long as I've got something white to wear under my choir robe, nobody will know the difference."

There was church on Sunday morning, and Jackie didn't find out till later that Gretchen had taken a novel along and read it all through the sermon. And after dinner, when the roast had been served not quite done, Jackie insisted that Gretchen wash her hair and straighten her room, and Gretchen became moody and sarcastic.

"I don't know how mother *stands* her! I really don't!" Jackie complained to her father as Gretchen clattered and banged overhead. "Was *I* ever like that, Dad?"

Mr. Cleaver smiled wisely. "The problems are always there," he grinned, "just different at different ages, that's all. Don't think we'll ever stop worrying about either of you. And if you have children, I suppose we'll go through it all over again."

Jackie frowned to herself as she spread her physics books out on the dining room table and tried to work on Monday's assignment. Dad talked as though they still worried about *her!* Good grief, weren't you supposed to have *some* sense by the time you reached sixteen?

She was conscious of somebody standing in the doorway and looked up to see Gretchen, arms folded, staring at her sullenly.

"Room's clean, hair's washed, and if the Great Madame Jacqualine doesn't mind, I'm going out on the stupid old porch."

Jackie suppressed a smile. "Go ahead."

The door banged after her, and Jackie returned to her books.

Sunday night supper was easy—leftover roast, left-over potatoes, store-bought pie.

"Dad and I are going to visit Mom again tonight while you're at youth fellowship," Jackie told her sister. "If you get home before we do, the key's in the mailbox. Sometimes they let visitors stay till ten on the weekends."

There was the sound of mini-bikes on the driveway, and Gretchen went out to talk with two boys Jackie couldn't stand. Snatches of conversation floated through the window, self-conscious quips and bright remarks, and Jackie writhed with the corniness of it all.

Just when Jackie felt she couldn't stand it any long-er, Gretchen stuck her head in the door and yelled, "I'm off to fellowship, Jackie." A moment later she was riding down the street on one of the mini-bikes, and Jackie held her breath as she watched them round a corner. Well, at least they were headed for church. Gretchen would be safe there.

She put on her sandals and was just starting out the door with her father when the phone rang. It was Sally.

"No, Gretchen's already left for fellowship," Jackie told her.

"But there isn't any meeting tonight! It was can-celled. Jim was supposed to call everybody."

"Well, no one called us. I suppose she'll be home soon, then," Jackie said. "I'll leave a note for her to call you when she gets in."

44

When she hung up, however, Jackie had second thoughts.

"Listen, Dad, I think I'd better stay home and wait for Gretchen," she said. "Tell Mom I'll be in tomorrow after school."

"Think Gretchen will be along soon?"

"Sure. You go on, and don't worry."

Jackie got a dress she was making and took it to the sewing machine in the dining room. Seven o'clock. By now, Gretchen should have found the church empty and started back home. On impulse, she dialed the number in the church basement. There was no answer.

She sat down at the machine again and worked on the facing. A car drove up, and she went to the window to look. Only the neighbors.

Seven-thirty came, and finally eight. Contrary as Gretchen was, Jackie knew she wouldn't purposely get into trouble. But what about those boys? Once Gretchen had accepted a ride on their bike, what could she do? What if there had been an accident? Was she carrying identification? What if the boys took her somewhere and wouldn't bring her home? What if, what if, what if!

She called Sally and two other friends of Gretchen's. No one had heard from her. Eight became nine, and then nine-thirty.

In desperation Jackie called the pastor and asked him to check the church. He called back five minutes later to say that the church was empty and there were no mini-bikes around.

She was near tears when the door opened at ten and there were footsteps in the hallway. With pounding

heart, she sat at the sewing machine and waited. The footsteps moved to the kitchen and the refrigerator door opened.

"Gretchen?"

"Yeah?"

Relief and fury flowed through her at the same time. Jackie got up and went to the kitchen, her lips pressed tightly together. Gretchen was making a pickle sandwich and added great globs of peanut butter to the top slice.

"Where have you been?"

"Out with Bill and Eddie. There wasn't any meeting tonight, but nobody told me."

She said it so simply, so innocently, that Jackie wanted to leap over and bang her head against the toaster.

"Why didn't you *call* me? Why didn't you come back home then?"

Gretchen looked up. " 'Cause I knew you'd be gone! You said you were going to the hospital."

"Well, I didn't go. Sally called, and I found out that the meeting was cancelled, and so I decided to wait for you."

"How was I supposed to know? Why didn't you go ahead?"

"Because I wanted to be sure you got home safely, that's why! What in the world have you been doing all this time? I was worried sick!"

Gretchen took a bite and licked her fingers. "Well, after we found the church locked, we went to the snack shop for a pizza. Then we rode around the

47

school on the mini-bikes for a while. When it started to sprinkle, we went to Bill's, and listened to records, and then we went to Leed's to see if any of the kids were there, and then I walked home. It's the same time I always get in from fellowship. We always go for pizza afterwards. I figured this was when you'd expect me."

This time Jackie's voice shook. "But I didn't *know* any of that. All I knew was that you left with Bill and Eddie on those stupid bikes, and I didn't know where. I was frantic!"

Gretchen stopped eating. "Jackie, listen!" she said. "You sound just like Mom! You really do! I mean, it's amazing! She's only been gone for three days, and you sound exactly like her!"

"Well, that's just the way it is!" Jackie cried. "And if you had the responsibility for someone else, you'd worry, too. You're not made of glass. Maybe *you* know you're all right, and *you* know you wouldn't get into trouble, but how do I know it unless you tell me? It's not enough just one person knowing. You've got to communicate. Because if I've got nothing more to go on than the things I see and hear, then I've got reasons to worry plenty, believe me!"

"Honest, Jackie, I didn't mean to get you all shook up. I mean it! From now on I'll let you in on everything I do. I promise. I wish you'd go blow your nose or something. You look like you're going to bawl!"

It was almost funny the way Gretchen said it. Jackie would have laughed if she wasn't so close to tears.

She went into the living room and blew her nose.

There were going to be some changes around here between her and Gretchen. And now that she knew how it was with Mom, she was going to make some promises herself.

That
O'Connell
Girl

Every March 17 I live it all over again. That's one of the things about growing up—you're old enough to realize how awful you once were. If only you could forget.

Back in third grade, St. Patrick's Day was a big deal. It wasn't that so many of us were Irish. It's just that it was a chance to break the monotony, and everybody wore something green to school, even kids with names like Feldstein, Waleski, and Wong.

Jean O'Connell was the only pure Irish girl among us. Maybe we resented her for that, I'm not sure. Every year since kindergarten, on St. Patrick's Day Jean O'Connell had come to school in more green than a golf course. She always wore a green skirt and sweater and socks, with a little shamrock pin that her grandmother had sent her from Dublin. In third grade the teacher asked if she knew any Irish songs, and she did. She got so much attention that some of us with mere English, French, and German blood in our veins were sorry that St. Patrick had ever gone to Ireland at all.

It was afterwards, in the lunchroom, that it happened. Jean O'Connell was passing out little green-sugared shamrock cookies from her lunch pail, and I said I didn't want any. Barbara and Lois decided they didn't either.

"They're good," Jean said invitingly. "I helped bake them yesterday. We always make them for St. Patrick's Day."

"And get them blessed by the Pope too, I'll bet," I said. Barbara and Lois giggled.

"What do you mean?" asked Jean. "What does the Pope have to do with it?"

I was getting to her, I could tell, and the venom inside me seemed to spread. What little I knew about Catholics—true or false, rumored or real—I dredged up for the big confrontation.

"I'll bet you'd have got him to bless them if you could," I said airily. "I'll bet you'd have crawled a mile on your knees just so he could spit on the cookies and make them blessed."

"She'd kiss his ring too," Lois said maliciously. "Don't forget the ring."

"You don't know what you're talking about," Jean said, hurt. "I never kissed anybody's ring in my life."

"You worship idols, though," Barbara said. "I've seen them. I went to a Catholic church once with my cousins, and there were big statues all around, and people lit candles for them and knelt down and everything."

"And you have to cross yourself with magic signs

and pray over beads and wear a cross around your neck," added Lois knowingly.

The green sugar cookies seemed to be turning bitter in Jean's mouth. She put the rest back into her lunch box. But we didn't know enough to stop.

"Yeah, you Catholics think you're better than anyone else," Barbara said. "You think that everybody else is heathen—nobody's going to heaven but you. Boy, I don't know how a church can be so stuck up."

Jean's voice trembled slightly. "I never said that about anyone." She shut her lunch box with a snap. "Whether you go to heaven or not is your business."

Later, I often thought what she could have said right then. It was a perfect opportunity to tell us off— to suggest that if this was any sample of our behavior, we weren't about to get there. But she didn't. She got up and walked out to the playground in her green socks and sweater and skirt, and Barbara and Lois and I grinned smugly at each other because that O'Connell girl finally got what was coming to her. Why she had it coming, we didn't exactly know. She was Catholic. Wasn't that enough?

Third grade quarrels never last long, however, and the following week we were all jumping rope together like always. But not exactly like always. I don't know just how to explain it. We didn't say anything more to Jean O'Connell about her being Catholic. We didn't even say much to each other about it. It was just the way I saw Jean look at us whenever Lois and Barbara and I were together, as though she suspected we were talking about her.

By fourth grade, I had practically forgotten what

I'd done in the third. I was learning to sew, to ride a horse—I was collecting buttons and tea cups and knitting a scarf for my sister. Jean O'Connell and I even went to the mountains together with the Campfire Girls, and she was friendly, as though nothing had ever happened.

When March 17 came, however, and we all put on our green socks or green ribbons, Jean O'Connell came to school in a navy blue jumper and white socks. She didn't even wear her pin from Dublin. When somebody asked her about it, she just shrugged and made a face. The teacher asked if anybody knew some Irish ballads, and when all the kids turned to Jean, she said she'd forgotten them.

"That's a shame," the teacher said warmly. "It's nice to value one's heritage, and the Irish have a wealth of songs and stories."

Jean said nothing. Neither did we.

The years went on—junior high, high school—and every so often our paths would cross again. Jean and I were on the student newspaper together, in the same gym class, the operetta, the senior play. She got her driver's license first, and once she even picked me up for play rehearsal.

The summer we graduated, Jean O'Connell got married to a law student. She was the first one of our crowd to marry, and we all wished her well. The wedding was to be in St. Mary's Cathedral, the newspapers said, and invitations had been sent. Other girls talked about going. But I received no invitation. Neither did Lois nor Barbara.

The day of the wedding came, and I thought how

silly it was that Jean should hold a grudge against us all these years. We were mere kids then. What did we know about Catholicism or prejudice or even manners?

I washed my hair and sat out on the patio to let it dry.

It bothered me more than I wanted it to. It bothered me that after all these years, Jean's hurt had never healed. I imagined how she looked coming down the aisle of St. Mary's in her white gown, with her rosary and prayer book. I could feel with her the solemnity of the moment, the importance of the setting, the value of her beliefs and traditions. . . .

And suddenly I knew that it wasn't pettiness that had kept Jean from inviting us. It was simply that she knew what we really thought of her church, her religion, and the customs she had been taught from the cradle on. And on this—her day, in this beautiful moment—she did not want things spoiled by a remembrance of how we had scoffed. She did not want her church desecrated by those of us who could only criticize. I closed my eyes, but I couldn't close out the memory.

What, over the years, had Jean thought about me? How did my own Christianity show up against hers? Was I, with my Protestant friends, an example of the joy and power that comes of knowing Jesus directly, or were we truly heathenlike, not only in our behavior, but in our hearts as well?

So what can you do? After all, we were only children. Kids just do awful things sometimes. Jean O'Connell had probably done her share of rude things too. Hadn't I been kind to her since? You can't go on forever feeling guilty about the dumb things you did in third grade.

Then I relived the evening that Jean had picked me up in her car and driven me to play rehearsal. I don't even remember what we were talking about. All I remember is that at one point in the conversation I felt it would have been a good opportunity to say something about that March 17 in third grade—to tell her I was sorry and that I had grown up a lot since then, to say that everybody should be free to discover God in her own way, and that I sincerely wished her well. But for some reason I didn't. For some reason I let it pass. For some reason I let her feelings about me and my own faith go uncorrected, and I could well imagine what her feelings were.

I stared up at the trees overhead and thought of how Jean was probably leaving the cathedral now, to start a new life with her husband. It could be a new chance for me too, I decided. I could resolve that from this day forward, I would not let my unkindnesses pass without apologizing. I would resolve to look for opportunities to bring understanding where there was prejudice, tolerance where there was bigotry. If I could succeed even a little in redirecting my life, that O'Connell girl will have helped me more than she'll ever know.

Starting Over

He rolled over on his back and was surprised by the scent of pine. He could still smell. Thank God for that. He was beginning to think that his whole body had become so jaded that his senses no longer functioned. He wondered if Lorraine had noticed it too.

She snuggled up beside him there on the blanket under the trees and traced his profile with one finger.

"What's the matter, lover?" she asked.

"Nothing." That described him and everything else. The nothingness, that overpowering sense of lack—lack of tenderness, of joy, of passion even. When had he and Lorraine become like zombies? Or had they ever really been so different?

She moved away from him then and returned to her side of the blanket, staring up at the stars. It was nothingness for her too, Doug knew, and yet she went on pretending it was great. The Academy Award—that's what she should get. That's what they both deserved.

Somehow he had thought that it would be different. The other guys always said how great it was. But the guys were always talking. By the time you were a senior in high school, you just sort of knew what they said was bluffing. But not all of it. Sex was *supposed* to be passion with a capital P, wasn't it? Nobody ever said a word about nothingness.

Somewhere a mockingbird ran through its repertoire high in one of the trees. Doug listened. He remembered, suddenly, that there had been a mockingbird the first time he had brought Lorraine here to the blanket in the park. For five months they had been coming here twice a week or so for the furtive grappling of bodies and the quick surge of pleasure. They pretended it was great and satisfying and Something Wonderful. Maybe it was—in the right situation with the right person. What it was with Lorraine was a habit.

He had wanted so much more. He had wanted a girl who really meant something to him, a girl that figured, somehow, in his future. He wanted to feel concern for her and joy that he had found her, as well as desire. All he felt for Lorraine was that she was the wrong girl—the whole situation was wrong. The feeling grew stronger each time they made out.

He wanted out. He wanted to enter another relationship slowly, with respect and concern. He could not do this with Lorraine, because they had started off a sham, and each time the facade seemed to grow thicker.

He sat up and rested his arms on his knees. It was difficult enough saying good-bye to a girl you had simply dated a few times but didn't want to see again.

How on earth did you say good-bye to someone when you'd been intimate, when she knew your body and you knew hers? Strange, he thought, they knew each other's bodies but they hadn't begun to know each other's minds or souls. They were perfect strangers on a spiritual level.

Doug was not one to pass the blame. He knew, though, that it was easier to become involved sexually now than it once was. Parents, too often mixed up sexually in their own lives, often refused to take a stand one way or another. Even some church people recognized that there were different life-styles, and that regardless of what you chose to be, you were still a child of God—which Doug believed too, with all his heart.

What all this meant, of course, was that the decision was squarely on his own shoulders—his and Lorraine's. They had made a choice, and it had been a foolish one. What on earth did he do now?

"Come on, Doug, let's have it. You haven't been yourself for several weeks. What's wrong? Something I can't cure?"

He smiled. "Yes," he answered, "something even you can't cure."

"Who is she, Doug? You can tell me. There were no strings attached."

Doug shook his head. "There's no other girl right now, Lorraine. It's just that something is missing from my life, and I need time to find it. Can you understand that?"

Lorraine looked at him a moment without speaking. "No, I can't. What more do you want? I thought you liked coming out here with me."

"Lorraine, you could be the queen of Sheba, and it wouldn't change how I feel right now. I'm looking for a deep relationship, something with meaning."

"Dougie boy's gone sober," Lorraine pouted.

"Maybe so."

"So what else are you looking for?"

"Passion."

"You've got it."

"Tenderness."

"So?"

"Joy."

She was silent. "You want the moon, buster."

"Maybe. I was always hard to please." He stood up, helped Lorraine to her feet, and folded up the blanket.

"Did you smell the pine tonight?" he asked curiously.

"What pine?"

"It's there. You have to sort of search it out with your senses. There's a lot to life that you have to really work for. Nothing that's beautiful comes easy."

They walked slowly back to the car, a yard apart, and Doug knew he would never bring her out here again. He felt sad for her, sad for himself, sad for a relationship that had been all wrong from the beginning.

"Well, Doug," she said as they reached the car, "it's been fun. Maybe we both need a change. So good luck, good health, and all that sort of thing. Just don't go gray over it."

Casual to the last. But it was easier this way. No, he wouldn't go gray over it. In fact, now that the decision had been made, he felt better about himself than he had in a long time. He was opening his life to a relationship with meaning, with respect, with honesty . . . a relationship that could go somewhere. He would replace the nothingness with joy, and he hoped that someday, with someone else, Lorraine would find it too.

Reflection

The heat seemed even more oppressive when she boarded the bus, and I watched in growing revulsion as she pulled her huge bulk up the steps and stood puffing against the coin meter.

"Gonna be another hot one," she said to the driver, who ignored her, swerving out into the road again as soon as she had deposited her token.

She lurched to the side seat behind him and lowered herself, huffing some more. Her monstrous legs bulged in the tight pants as her thighs flattened against the cushion.

"Whew!" she smiled, looking gregariously about. "Bet you could fry an egg on the sidewalk today."

I quickly turned my head to the view outside and noticed others doing the same, as if her grossness were contagious. My eyes, however, kept traveling across the aisle to the seat at the front, hoping each time I looked that she might have miraculously disappeared.

She smelled of sweat and cheap perfume, and the peach-colored powder on her face ended in a line around her jaw. It was not only her size, I decided, but her artificiality that seemed so repelling. Her tired, bleached hair showed black at the roots, and pendulous earrings of pink and green glass hung grotesquely down each side of her thick neck. Her eyes seemed half hidden by the swelling of fat on her cheeks, and her orange lipstick had smeared onto her chin, as though she were bleeding from the gums.

She leaned over the railing, till her head almost touched the driver's.

"Don't seem like the bus is air-conditioned so good today."

"Same's it always is," the driver responded. "You just can't feel it, that's all."

His sarcasm went unnoticed. "I sure don't have no trouble feelin' the heat!" she said. "Seems like it's been ninety 'most four days now."

Picking up a newspaper on the seat, she began to fan herself, the flesh rolling and bobbing on the underside of her arm. Her pink stretch blouse crept up over the top of her slacks to reveal a layer of fat pinched between her garments, and when I dropped my eyes, embarrassed, I was confronted with her feet, misshapen by bunions, which bulged out the openings in her sandals.

"You get over to the bay much?" she asked the driver. "We was over the other night. Not too hot at night."

For a moment the driver didn't answer. Then he said irritably, "Look, lady, I got to drive this bus." And the huge woman fell silent.

After several blocks, she opened her purse and

pulled out an astrology guide, slumping over and holding it up close to her face. Each new position she assumed seemed uglier than the last. How, I wondered, had she become this way? Surely she hadn't always been so repulsive. Somewhere as a young woman or even a child, she must have had a certain natural charm about her, hidden now by layers of fat and peach-colored powder and innumerable home peroxides. At what point did the falseness creep in? At what year had she become gross? And how did she view herself, this woman in the tight clothes and the horrid glass earrings and the sickening cheap perfume?

She closed her astrology book and leaned toward the driver again.

"I'm a Pisces," she confided. "I'm supposed to be cautious of strangers today. What are you?"

"A stranger, lady," the driver barked.

Someone across the aisle laughed. The fat woman looked around and laughed too, somewhat self-consciously.

"I'm a Pisces," she said again to the passengers, now that she had their attention. "Last week the stars said I was going to have trouble with relatives and my sister came over and I thought it meant trouble, but she came bringin' me a pecan cake. Now what do you think of that?"

"I think you've had too much cake," said another man, and this time several others laughed with him.

The woman blushed and turned back to the driver. "Sometimes the stars are right and sometimes they ain't," she sighed. He did not answer. The bus lumbered on, and the heavy woman swayed sideways, the fat jiggling furiously under her chin. And then, as if to assuage her loneliness, she reached into her purse for a package of gum. With fat fingers she unwrapped two sticks, rolled them into a ball, and deposited them in her orange mouth. With eyes half-closed, she settled back in the seat, her knees wide apart, ankles crossed, and her big jowls working up and down as she snapped and sucked at the gum.

The bus approached the bridge and the woman made no move to get off. She would be riding at least as far as Meadow Heights, I realized, and I felt a definite resentment toward her. It was as though she were purposely trying to be repugnant, sitting there with her fat legs sprawled on the seat, her gum snapping, her perfume penetrating the air. Why should our ride be unpleasant because of this useless lump of flesh, whose only function, it seemed, was to gorge itself?

The bus stopped at the bridge for a young mother with a baby, who deposited her fare and sank wearily down in the seat opposite the fat woman. Instantly the sound of gum snapping was replaced by the baby's whine. For a few blocks it was only an irritable fuss, but as the bus rolled on up the hill, it became louder and more insistent.

The mother picked the child up so he could see out the window, but he threw back his head, banging it against her arm, and howled. Embarrassed, the young woman tried clapping his hands together and bouncing him on her knee. Each new effort brought louder screaming. The child kicked and struggled, caught up in the paroxysm of his fatigue.

The mother looked helplessly about in apology. "I don't know what's the matter with him today," she said, bewildered.

The male passengers stared stonily out the windows, frowning slightly.

"He's tired, and it's so hot," a woman in the third row volunteered, and went back to her newspaper.

The shrieking now had a piercing quality. In staccato rhythm the yells started and stopped, started and stopped, as though the child were trapped in a pattern he could not escape.

The bus was reaching Meadow Heights, and the big woman behind the driver pulled herself to her feet with one fat hand. Slowly she inched across the aisle, until she reached the mother and child, grasping the overhead strap.

She bent down till she was just above the child and smiled at him with puffy eyes. The screams died out as the baby surveyed this strange new face so close to him.

"I know just how you feel, honey," she said. "It's been a rough day for me too. Bet you could fry an egg on that sidewalk."

With her left hand she removed one of her pendulous earrings and dangled it before the little boy. The cheap strands of pink and green glass caught the sun and sparkled, twisting and turning with the roll of the bus, sending shimmers of light around and around in a mad sort of merry-go-round.

Eagerly the child reached up, stretching his little

arm till his fingers closed at last over the earring, and with a happy grunt he shook his fist up and down.

"Maybe that'll keep him happy till you get home." The huge woman smiled and moved toward the exit.

"Oh, no. . . . I couldn't . . . !" the mother said quickly.

"Didn't cost but a few pennies," said the woman. "I'll never miss it." Edging her way down the steps, she climbed off the bus, and the door closed after her, shutting out forever the sight and sound of her and the smell of her cheap perfume.

"Her earring!" the young mother said in amazement, looking about. "She gave him one of her earrings!" She looked down at her child, who was resting quietly against her, examining the new plaything with rapt attention, absorbed in the brilliance of the pink and green glass.

The Witness

There was something vaguely unsettling about the meeting that night, all the more so because everyone else was so enthused.

"Wasn't it great, Evie?" Gwen said as they walked outside into the spring air. "You know, I don't think I've ever been in a group that thinks and feels so much alike. When Ted read that piece on ecology, I felt as if all of us were saying *Amen* in unison."

That was it exactly—one big happy, educated, and aware youth fellowship, talking to itself. You knew how people felt before they got up to speak. You knew what they would say before they even opened their mouths. And you agreed with them in advance, because all hearts beat as one.

Evelyn said goodbye at the corner and walked the last block alone, drinking in the fragrance of hyacinths from someone's garden. It wasn't the first time she had felt this way. Sometimes, on Sunday mornings, the thought was overwhelming. Sometimes, when the sermon was especially good, it seemed that the pastor was saying what they already knew, the choir was singing to itself, and everyone was agreeing with everyone else.

What was bothering her, anyway? Wasn't a church a fellowship of like-minded Christians who gathered together to encourage and inspire one another?

Evelyn opened the front door and went on up to her room, her brown hair tangled from the wind. Yes, she told herself, that was part of it, certainly. The church school classes, her teachers, her faith had sustained her through many difficult times and helped her make countless decisions about her life. But the other part was reaching out to people who hadn't yet felt that surge of awareness, of dedication and purpose. A church that did only half a job still had a long way to go.

What kind of Christian was she, anyway? Her Bible lay on her dresser, well read. Her desk was covered with folders of youth fellowship projects in which she was involved. A scrapbook on her bedside stand was filled with mementos of countless church and choir activities. And yet?

She saw him the moment she walked into fellowship the following Sunday. Like a tin can on a grand piano, he seemed terribly out of place somehow, possibly because he looked so uncomfortable.

Evelyn had seen him before—this rather unattractive hunk of brawn, lumbering about the soccer field at school—but she had no idea who he was or why he was here. He stood with his hands in his pockets, ill-at-ease. The other two members who had arrived earlier were bustling about in a flurry of activity, as if being busy could substitute for conversation.

"Hi," Evelyn said, walking over, embarrassed at the awkwardness. "I'm Evie Eastman."

"Matt Kline," the boy answered. "Just . . . uh . . . thought I'd drop by. Ted Convis invited me. Said if I wasn't busy sometime I might wanta come over."

"We're glad you could make it. Did Ted know you were coming tonight? He's out of town for the week-end."

A flush spread slowly up Matt's neck, and he shifted his weight to the other foot. "I guess I shoulda called him first. I was . . . just . . . you know . . . going by."

"You're welcome any time," Evelyn said quickly. "Come on. Let's go meet the others."

"Live around here, Matt?" one of the fellows asked when Evelyn had introduced them.

"Over in McClean Gardens," Matt answered.

It figured. McClean Gardens was a new development, built to provide housing for low-income families. It was part of the community in location only—a huge, spreading complex of buildings like an army camp, and Evelyn had never thought much about the people inside it.

All the while she was talking to Matt, trying desperately to keep a conversation going, she was fighting the feelings that rose up inside her, as if they belonged to someone else: *Why doesn't he just leave and say he'll be back sometime when Ted's here? When will he realize he's just out of place? How can he possibly fit in? This is an intelligent group, used*

70

to serious discussions and debates. There's simply nothing here to interest him....

"Good grief, Ted will invite anybody," Gwen said as the two girls went to the church kitchen to get some coffee started. "I've seen this guy around at school, I think, but he talks like he never finished seventh grade."

"He lives in McClean Gardens," Evelyn told her, and then was sorry that she had. It labeled him.

"Oh," Gwen said knowingly. "I suppose we'll be getting more of them, won't we?"

Them. Who was "them"? *The opposite of "we,"* Evelyn thought as she went back to the fellowship room and sat down across the aisle from Matt. *If "we" are intelligent and witty and educated and aware, then Matt is . . . ?* Strange, she was thinking, but if Matt had been black, or Indian, or Hindu, or Russian, the group would have gone out of its way to make him feel welcome. But because he was a "greaser," with a different sort of upbringing, they all wished he would just fade quietly away.

The service consisted of readings from the Bible and *The Prophet*, and some poems by Walt Whitman. They were beautifully done by Gwen and Steve and Kenny. Out of the corner of her eye, Evelyn watched Matt. Like a fidgety cat, he leaned forward, arms resting on his knees, cracked his knuckles, looked up at the ceiling, sat up straight again, crossed his feet, uncrossed them, wound his watch, leafed through the hymnal, and rested his arms on his knees again.

A discussion followed the readings. Everyone had something to say—except Matt, who remained silent.

Even when they broke up later for coffee and brownies, it was hard to draw him into the conversation. In-jokes had to be explained. Matt sat awkwardly in a chair at the outer edge of the circle, smiling constantly in an effort to be one of the group, but the smile was strained, and it made him seem all the more distant and separate. And when the meeting finally ended, everyone was relieved that Matt left immediately so they wouldn't have to invite him to go with them for pizza, a Sunday night tradition.

It was when they were sitting at Tony's, six to a booth, that Evelyn saw him pass the window and glance inside. It was such a fleeting glance she could not be sure he had seen them. And yet, somehow she felt that he had. He knew that, despite all the polite words, they hadn't really meant them. He was welcome to come to their church, but not to be a part of it. Not really. Not any more than McClean Gardens was part of the community.

"A pox on it all!" Evelyn said to herself the next day, trudging home from school with an armload of books. "Ted should have made sure he'd be there before he invited Matt. It's up to him to make Matt feel at home, not us."

But somehow, her excuses just didn't stick. What kind of Christian was she, anyway? The question kept coming back. What kind of witness? She wasn't the type who could stand on a street corner and ask the passing throng if they knew Jesus. Anyone could stand on the street and pass out tracts to folks they would never see again. Witnessing, Evelyn always believed, meant getting involved in another's life. It meant showing, by one's own example, that Christ's teachings were worth believing. And ultimately it meant persuading another that there was a place for him in the congregation and that he was needed.

This church hadn't even gone out to get Matt. He had come to them. And they had extended their hands half-heartedly, waiting for Ted to come back and do the job for them. And Matt knew. Oh, how he knew!

"I'm going to McClean Gardens for a while, Mother," Evelyn said as soon as dinner was over. "I know someone there. Be back soon."

"Maybe you'd better phone and we'll come pick you up," her mother suggested. "I don't especially want you there after dark."

The unspoken prejudice. Not once, as far as Evelyn knew, had there been any crimes committed in McClean Gardens, yet everyone assumed, because the incomes were low. . . .

Walking into the large courtyard, Evelyn realized she had no idea where to find Matt. She checked the mail boxes inside the first apartment building. There was no Kline listed. She went back outside and was starting toward the office when she saw a familiar figure coming across the open space, dressed in a sweatshirt and carrying a jacket over one shoulder.

"Hi," she said going up to him.

Matt stopped and stared at her in the half-darkness.

"Oh . . . hi!" he said, in a mixture of surprise and embarrassment. "What you doin' over here?"

Evelyn smiled. "A girl will do anything to lose a few

pounds, and when I found out you lived so close, I decided to walk over instead of call."

"Yeah? What's up?"

"We need your help, that's what." The words came more easily than she'd thought they would. "Look, I'm in charge of a project our fellowship is doing with handicapped children at the Fowler School. We want to offer them two hours a week of physical activities and arts and crafts. Almost everybody volunteered for arts and crafts and hardly anybody for physical ed. We'd love to have you help out. I've seen you on the soccer field, and I know you'd do a great job teaching them a few sports."

Matt shifted uneasily. "Oh . . . I don't know. . . ."

"You wouldn't need anything special," Evelyn said quickly. "Just patience, understanding, dependability, dedication. . . ."

"Some kind of saint, huh?"

They both laughed.

"Sort of," said Evelyn. "Seriously, Matt, we'd love to have you join in. We need you. We really do."

"Well . . . I don't know. . . ."

"Look. Would you just do this? Come to a planning meeting Thursday night at Tony's Pizza Shack. The pizza's on me."

Matt grinned. "Sure," he said, mimicking her. "A guy will do anything for a pizza."

"Good!" Evelyn laughed. "I'll remember that. See you, then, at Tony's."

She turned and started back across the courtyard. Suddenly, Matt's voice rang out behind her, clear and sharp:

74

"It's gonna louse you up, you know. Unless you're just a phony."

Evelyn stopped, her heart in her mouth.

"What?" she asked, turning around.

"It's gonna louse up your diet, isn't it? No use walkin' all the way over here if you're gonna put it back on again eatin' pizza." His eyes were laughing.

Evelyn laughed too. "Matt, I am a phony. You might as well know. I figured you'd be more likely to say yes if I asked you face to face. That's why I came over."

"Well," he smiled. "At least you're honest about it. See you Thursday, then."

"Seven o'clock," Evelyn said. "And don't be late, or it'll be all gone by the time you get there."

The Prime
of Life

I'd always thought of Dad, see, as . . . well, the big guy who got up every morning and drove to the Department of Agriculture. He was more than that, of course. He was the man who played table tennis with me on winter evenings and rode bikes with me in summer along the C & O canal and ate peanut butter and onion sandwiches. A two-legged credit card, the guy at the head of the table, a balding tenor in the church choir, and an amateur plumber. I mean, I never really thought about him much. He just *was*.

I suppose you could say I took him for granted, but the reason I never worried about whether he was fulfilled or not was that I figured he liked what he was doing or he wouldn't be doing it. If fighting his way through rush hour traffic for an hour and a half to get to work and doing the same thing to get home again was his bag, who was I to stop him? If carting the family off to Ocean City every summer and Pennsylvania for Christmas was what turned him on, why should I complain? And so we sort of went through the days and weeks and months together in syncopated rhythm, each to his own concerns, Mom and Dad and Davie and me.

And then one day I came home from school to find Dad there—in the middle of the afternoon, yet—and he and Mom were sitting at the dining room table with maps and papers and a pot of coffee. Dad—old stickin-the-mud, take-'im-for-granted Dad—was talking a mile a minute, and his face was flushed like a little kid who just got a fire engine for Christmas. I stood in the doorway a full minute before he noticed me— *me*, his sixteen-year-old wonder son! And then he turned with a grin as wide as his hand and said, "Bert, how would you like to go to Utah?"

What could I say? Mountains to climb, horses to ride, copper mines, spruce trees, and the Mormon Tabernacle Choir!

"Great!" I said. "What are you doing? Planning our vacation?"

"Nope," says Dad, and he drew out his words slowly. "I'm going to sell this place and move us all to Utah."

I looked at him like he'd gone mad.

"*Move?*" I croaked. "Leave Washington, D.C.? Leave the Department of Agriculture?" I couldn't believe it. And when Dad kept nodding, I got down to the heart of the matter. "Leave my *friends?* My *school?*"

When I saw that Dad was serious, I collapsed on a chair and stared helplessly at Mother. "What's he going to do in Utah, Mom? Be a mountain guide?"

But even Mom had that faraway look in her eye. "No," she said dreamily. "Raise sheep."

"Sheep!" I bleated, even sounding like one. "We're going halfway across the continent to raise sheep? Dad, you're going bananas! You really are!"

"Listen, Bert," said Mother. "this is something your father has wanted to do all his life, and he finally got the chance. A man from work is selling his ranch and offered it to us. Your father is going to retire from the government early and do the things he's always wanted. We're leaving the first of July, so it's not as if we're going tomorrow. You'll have plenty of time to do things with your friends before then."

As the days wore on, I clutched at straws. Maybe it wouldn't be so bad, living on a ranch. I imagined a long, low, redwood ranch house with a stone fireplace. But when I brought it up with Dad, he showed me a picture of a little pillbox house surrounded by acres and acres of flat country, with mountains in the background and, of course, sheep. Baaa.

My first thought was that I could break a leg—maybe both legs—and have to be in George Washington Hospital for a year, so Dad would call off the deal. Then I decided that they'd probably just tie me, casts and all, to a luggage rack on top of the car, and drive me to Utah anyway.

So I tried getting morose and moody. Maybe they'd think I was going psychotic, the shock of leaving my friends and all that, but they were so full of plans that they didn't even notice.

I asked them if I could finish out my last two years of high school with my friend Jim but they reminded me that Jim's parents had only three bedrooms and five kids, and besides, Dad would need me on our so-called ranch.

April became May, and May, June. I went to picnics and parties with the gang like a condemned man on his last night out. I treasured the faces of all the girls I knew, knowing I would never see them again. I even wrote down some of Jim's corny jokes so I'd have them to cheer me up when I was a captive on that Utah ranch.

I finally faced the fact—that when a man reaches a certain age, he doesn't care about his oldest begotten son anymore. It didn't bother him that he was stunting my emotional maturity and thwarting my social life by separating me from my friends. Duty and responsibility had been replaced with rams and ewes, and I was simply another ranch hand separated from the outside world in those caverns between the mountains.

Two years—that's all I wanted—just enough time to finish high school and graduate. Then I'd be off to college and they could go to Utah and breed all the sheep they wanted. You'd think Dad would have thought of that. You'd think he would have thought of all of us, not just himself. But July 1 couldn't come any too soon for him, and every morning he started out on his smog-filled journey to the Department of Agriculture, he counted the days he had left before he'd be free.

A couple weeks before we left, the guys gave me a sort of farewell dinner. We gathered at Pogo's Pizza Palace, and they all chipped in and bought me an extra large with anchovies and a mug of root beer. We were all talking about what we wanted to do eventually, or more to the point, what we didn't (herd sheep, for instance). Mac said he wanted to travel through South America on a motor bike, and Jim wanted to ski in the Alps. I said I'd always wanted to fly a plane, and Eddie wanted to go on safari in Africa. All the guys agreed that we'd better make our dreams real before age forty because our lives would be half over by then. And we sort of joined hands over the anchovies and made a pact that we'd all call each other on our thirty-ninth birthdays and remind each other that we had one year left.

That night I got to thinking about what the guys had said, especially that part about life being half over at forty. Good grief, my dad was close to fifty, and what had he got out of life so far? Eight thousand nine hundred and thirty-one (I figured it out) trips to downtown Washington and the Department of Agriculture, fourteen trips to Ocean City, nine to Pennsylvania, and a couple hundred peanut butter and onion sandwiches. All these years he had plodded along so Davie and Mom and I could have the things we needed. All these years he'd slaved so I could enjoy my friends and parties and do my own thing. And suddenly, here was his chance, in the later years of his life, to do the thing he'd always wanted—to escape the smog-filled beltway and the reserved parking places and get out to the West where his soul could drink in the mountains and clouds and the huge expanse of space.

What were two years to me—the guy who had a

lifetime ahead to learn to fly, if that's what I wanted? But two years to Dad may be two of the few good years he had to live his life as he'd always wanted, and what was I doing to encourage him? Bleating all over the place, that's what.

I woke up Saturday morning to the fact that Sunday was Father's Day. So I went to a sporting goods store and bought Dad a ten-gallon hat and set it at his plate Sunday morning.

"For crying out loud!" Dad said when he found it, and he looked real pleased. "Saddle me up, boys, and I'm ready to go. Now all we need is a horse, Bert. First thing we're going to buy when we get to Utah. One comes with the ranch, but we'll need another so you can ride along. And dogs. We've got to have some good sheep dogs."

Davie, my ten-year-old brother, was jumping all over the place. I mean, Davie would take a dog over a girl any day, so he didn't even know what he was missing.

"It was real thoughtful of you, Bert," Dad said, trying the hat on for size. "I know you're not real keen on going—it's pretty hard to break away from your crowd when a guy's your age—but a couple more years and you'll be in college and can do as you like. When this offer came, I had to take it or leave it. It was too good to pass up."

"I understand, Dad," I said, hoping I really did.

Which is why I'm sitting in the back of the station wagon right now on my way to Utah, writing this on the top of a suitcase and listening to Davie singing, "Home on the Range." And why I'm glad I didn't break both legs and end up in George Washington Hospital for a year. Besides, after being cooped up in this car with Davie for five days and cramming my legs between a suitcase and the ice chest, even Utah will look good, and I just might get along with those mountains after all.

Seventy
Times
Seven

The breakup was only two days old, but Doug felt as if he'd aged a year. When he woke on the third day, however, he realized that anger was creeping in where only pain had been before. He was glad.

Welcome to the club, he told himself, splashing water on his face. *About time you saw her for what she really is.*

What was it that had attracted him in the first place? The answer was easy. Beauty, figure, long straight hair shiny as glass. Judith had flirted with him the way a girl does when she wants a guy to notice her, and Doug had noticed. He remembered the first long walk they'd taken around the shopping mall—the way he'd playfully caught her hand, the way she smiled. Love was blind, and he was the blindest.

He hung the towel on the rack and dressed for school. He had overlooked her love of expensive places and presents as easily as if she had sneezed and said, "Excuse me." She was a high class girl, he'd told himself. Could she help it if she had good taste? He often asked her where she'd like to go for the evening, and she was only being honest when she suggested the most expensive restaurants. He had even taken on an extra part-time job at the drugstore to pay for it all.

One evening when he'd come home and sprawled exhausted on the rug, his mother had said, "If Judith had any feelings about you, she would see that you're working yourself to death."

Now, as he sat down to breakfast, he avoided his mother's eyes, but she asked the question he was dreading most.

"Did she give the bracelet back, Doug?"

"No." Doug took a deep breath and finally looked her in the face. "It was my mistake for even mentioning it to her, Mom, and I'm sorry. If you want, I'll call her mother and see if she can persuade Judith to give it back."

Mother pressed her lips together. "No," she said finally. "It's been painful enough for you already. Let's let it go, and chalk it up to experience."

"I'm sorry, Mom. I really am. . . ."

All the way to school Doug relived that hostile scene with Judith. During the summer, she had been given a lead part in a community theater group, and had portrayed a young girl in the 1890s. "If I could just find some old jewelry to go with my costume," Judith had pouted. Instantly Doug had thought of the antique bracelet his mother owned, and convinced her to loan it to Judith.

Judith had looked fantastic in the play, and the

bracelet added the finishing touch to her dress. But once the performance was over, Judith did not offer to give it back. When Doug tactfully mentioned it a week later, Judith insisted indignantly that she understood it was a gift, not a loan, that so many people had complimented her on it she couldn't possibly return it, and what's more, she thought he had a lot of nerve in asking.

One thing seemed to lead to another. As the weeks went by Judith began sniping at him about other things. He never took her any place new, she said. He never bought her anything *nice*. The seats they had at the last rock concert were perfectly awful, and if he really cared about her, he'd get nothing but the best. And then, the very first week of school, she had dropped him for somebody else, and seemed to take great pleasure in telling him goodbye.

He reached the school, threw his jacket into the locker, and went to his first class, still angry. As he passed Pete Henderson in the hall, Pete remarked, "Man, you don't just break up with a girl, do you, Doug. You make an enemy!"

"What do you mean?" Doug asked, but Pete was already late for chemistry.

It wasn't till noon that Doug realized what Judith was saying about him. He had just finished his sandwich and was starting on his pie when Jack Perona stopped by his table.

"Hey, Doug," he said playfully, "what's this I hear about you being such a tightwad that you always get the cheapest tickets when you take a girl anywhere?

What's the matter between you and Judith, man? Can't keep up with her?"

The anger which had been building up inside Doug since that morning overwhelmed him. Before he could answer, someone else came to talk to Jack, and finally the two boys moved off.

Doug shoved his pie away, picked up his books, and set out for the gym with long, heavy strides, trying to work out the fury in every step. What had he ever seen in Judith? She was nothing but a gold digger. Well, two could play this game. He'd tell the gang what she was really like. In fact, he'd tell them about the bracelet and how she literally stole it from his mom. He'd tell how she needled presents out of him he couldn't afford, nagged to go to the most expensive places. He'd fix her. He'd make it so no guy in school would want to date her.

He threw his body into the calisthenics, took his turn on the trampoline, and attacked the punching bag with a vengeance. One, two, three, four, five, six, seven. . . .

Seventy times seven flashed through his mind. *How often shall my brother sin against me, and I forgive him? Peter had asked. Seven times? And Jesus had answered, seventy times seven. . . .*

And suddenly Doug remembered one fleeting moment when he and Judith were leaving a restaurant. He had found her staring at her reflection in a mirrored wall. For a moment she seemed a fearful insecure girl, anxious about her looks, afraid, perhaps, that there was nothing at all worth loving beneath that beautiful exterior.

Somehow he knew that life wasn't always going to be so easy for Judith. Sometime someone would do to her what she had done to Doug, and she would feel all the agony he was feeling now. He was surprised to find that his anger was mixed with a touch of pity.

The coach blew the whistle for showers. Doug let the hot water stream over his aching muscles. Judith was saying what she did because she felt guilty—of that he was sure. There was no need for him to lower himself to that level. Let her say what she would, the truth would win eventually.

As he headed toward the Sweet Shop after school, Cindy Ellis caught up with him.

"I don't suppose it's any of my business, Doug," she said, "but what's happened between you and Judith? Gee, the things she's saying about you! She's telling the whole school you're a prize cheapskate."

Doug smiled a little. "I'm sorry she feels that way," he said. "Do you believe her?"

"No. I just thought you might like equal time to sound off."

"No thanks. I don't get my kicks like that," Doug said, and opened the door for her.

Cindy gave him a quick glance. "You're cool, Doug, you know it? I'd think you'd be seething."

"I've got better things to do with my time," he answered.

"Such as?"

"Such as buying a Coke for a pretty girl in a green skirt. I'll even be a big spender and throw in a scoop of ice cream."

Cindy laughed. "No, thanks. A Coke'll be fine. It's the company I enjoy."

"Same here," said Doug, and they sat down across from each other in the booth.

Making
the Break

It would have been easier, Anne thought, to have left home some night after everyone had gone to bed —to walk out past the henhouse and garden, down the road to the cluster of mailboxes, and catch the bus that came through on the way to Cincinnati.

Not that she didn't want to tell her mother good-bye or thank her father for her tuition or joke with her brothers. It was faces she preferred not to see, or rather the feelings behind those faces. For a long time she had known exactly what her family was thinking—family and relatives, too. They didn't have to say a word. But they did. Plenty.

Back in eighth grade was when it started.

"The math club?" Mother had said. "Why would you want to join something like that? Don't they have a future homemakers club?"

Anne had shrugged. "I just like fooling around with numbers, Mom. They do all kinds of things in the math club—puzzles, theories—it's exciting."

In ninth grade, math gave way to science, and in

90

tenth grade, Anne entered a science fair and won second prize.

"It's a whole new world, Dad," she tried to explain one night when her father came home from the quarry. "It's like being on the brink of discovery. Experiments are so much fun!"

"Well, if it's a hobby that amuses you, I don't see any harm in it," her father had said, leaning back in his chair and turning on the evening news.

Anne's younger brothers, of course, did not really care what she did. But they assumed. Any boy who came to the house to see her, in their eyes, was a potential husband, because that's what big sisters in this community had always done: gone to high school, dated, and married.

Relatives assumed the same thing. "She'll be married before she's twenty," Aunt Esther said to Mother one night, in earshot of Anne. "A popular girl like her won't have any trouble at all finding a nice young man and settling down."

But Mother had sighed. "I don't know," she had replied. "Anne has a mind of her own."

Gradually the family came to see that Anne was not what they expected her to be, and Anne began to feel she was somehow a disappointment.

"I want to go to the technological school in Cincinnati after I graduate," she had announced one evening at dinner, and the family had stared at her, speechless.

"Why on earth, Anne?" her mother had asked. "It's mostly boys who go to schools like that."

"Probably why she wants to go!" chorused Johnny and Sam.

"I want to get a degree in science," Anne told them. "I'd like to get a job in a laboratory doing research."

Father had frowned. "Aren't any laboratories around here, Anne, 'cept the one that makes soap."

"It wouldn't be here," said Anne. "Maybe it would be in Chicago or out in California."

Mother had put down her fork. "Chicago! California! You don't mean you'd move there!"

"I couldn't very well commute," Anne had said dryly. "I'd just have to see what kind of offer I got after I graduated. That's a long way off."

"But all our relatives are here, Anne!"

"How come it's got to be science?" her father questioned, puzzled. "Esther's girls didn't get any ideas like that. Sharon's teaching school here in the county, and Louise is a dietitian over at the hospital. Plenty of things you could do like that."

"What's so *different* about me?" Anne had exclaimed, hurt and angry. "What's so strange about a career in science?"

"Well, there'd be a lot of competition from a lot of smart boys," said Dad.

"So?" Anne had said. "Am I so dumb you're afraid I'll flunk out?"

No, that wasn't it. Nobody really seemed to know what was wrong. It was strange; it was different. Nobody had done it before, least of all a girl. The Millers were a close-knit group. They didn't make waves—didn't do outlandish things. They didn't argue much, either. So they agreed to let Anne go. She knew she had won, but the victory was not sweet. Her family was puzzled and silent, and Anne, in return, resented their lack of understanding. They were kind; they were helpful; but they did not encourage her.

And so the morning of Anne's departure arrived. She got out of bed as the gray dawn filled the room, and went down to the kitchen. This afternoon they would all walk down the road with her and wait for the bus. Mother was already up, making biscuits at the old stove, and Anne could hear the sound of her father's voice outside, talking to the hens as he always did when he scattered feed. She sat down at the table and watched her mother work.

"You're up already," Mother said. "Must be the smell of the fried ham that woke you."

"That and old Toby," said Anne. "That rooster could wake the dead. Do you suppose I'll be able to sleep without the sound of chickens in the morning?"

"I imagine you'll have to get used to a lot of things you didn't expect," Mother said, and Anne wished she hadn't mentioned it.

Father came in, saw Anne, smiled—not very convincingly—and washed his hands at the sink.

"Well, guess this is the last time I'll be sitting down to breakfast with my daughter for a long time," he said. And then, unable to contain it any longer, he turned to her and asked, "You *sure* you want to go through with this, honey? You don't *have* to catch that bus if you don't want. . . ."

He came over and sat down across from her.

Anne looked at her parents. How could she get

through to them? What could she say on this last morning to help them understand?

"Dad," she said finally, "do you remember the story you told me about your great-grandfather?"

Her father put down his coffee cup and tried to follow the change of topic. "Must have told you lots of stories about him, honey. Which one was that?"

"A long time ago you told me that all the Millers settled in Michigan and planted some apple orchards, remember?"

"Sure, I remember."

"And that all the Miller boys and girls, one after another, stayed in Michigan and worked the orchards, generation after generation—the women running the village store and making apple butter, and the men in the orchards."

"Sure."

"And then great-grandpa was born, and from the time he was a little kid, he never liked apples."

Her parents both laughed at the memory, and Mother put the platter of scrambled eggs on the table.

"What my great-grandfather was interested in, you told me, was machines, and what he wanted to do more than anything else was buy himself a quarry and dig limestone. And then he had his chance, so he moved down here to Indiana, and everybody acted as if he had done something awful. No one could understand why he had to be different, but you always said you were glad he did, that you and your brothers and your father were happy here."

For a long time Anne's father stared at her across

the table. At last he reached over and squeezed her hand.

"Okay, honey. I want you to go with my blessing. One part of me says, 'Stay home, Annie,' and the other part says, 'Go ahead.' There always have to be folks who are willing to strike out and take a chance, to follow a dream. And I want you to have yours."

Mother was smiling too, a more relaxed smile than Anne had seen for some time.

"We always said she resembled her great-grandfather, didn't we? I guess we'd forgotten about the adventuresome part."

"It's more than an adventure, Mom," Anne promised. "It's the career I was born for. There's a big wide world out there, with new discoveries being made every day. I'll never be really happy unless I have a part in it, but I'll never forget the way home. You can count on that."

Of Mozart
and a Good
Mechanic

It had been going on now for at least a year. Larry wondered how it ever got started. Maybe it had been coming all along.

He sat by his bedroom window, watching the snow pile up on the ledge, flake after flake, slowly building up the inch that the weather forecast had promised. That was the way it was with him and his folks. Nothing had happened all at once. It was just one small remark on top of another that had got them where they were now. They were all guilty.

Actually, it was in junior high when the first flare-up took place. He had come home from school with the assignment to read something by Shakespeare.

"Shakespeare!" his father had said. "That's what's wrong with the schools. Kids are supposed to be learning reading, writing, and numbers, and instead those half-brain teachers have them reading poetry and stuff."

"Shakespeare was considered primarily a play-wright," Larry had replied. He remembered just how

97

he had replied too. He remembered the tone of voice and the sneer on his face and the sort of sardonic smile on his lips.

"I don't care who he was, reading Shakespeare isn't going to teach you how to find a job or earn a living," his father had shot back, his anger instantly ignited.

And Larry remembered how he had taken out *The Complete Works of Shakespeare* from the library and read not one but two plays. He did not keep it up in his room, either, where he usually put his books, but on the stand in the living room on top of *Sports Illustrated* and *Modern Mechanics* so that every time his father wanted to read a magazine, he had to pick up that three-pound book first. That was how it all began.

And then last year, after listening to Mozart's fortieth symphony in music appreciation class, Larry had been so taken with it that he impulsively bought a recording of it for his mother for her birthday. He knew it would be strange to her, but he thought they could listen to it together, and he'd tell her what to listen for, the way the teacher had done with the class —repetitions of melodies that made it all come alive.

Mom had opened her presents with the radio blasting out country music in the background, and had stared at the record as if it must be a mistake. "Mo - - zart?" she had asked, fumbling over the pronunciation. "Say, what is this?"

And Larry, eager to explain how beautiful it was, turned off the radio and put the record on the phonograph, and the family sat woodenly around the dining room table. The first movement wasn't even half over before they began to get restless, Larry could tell.

98

Bob, his brother, had snickered finally and said, "*Fortieth* symphony? He should have quit after number one." That made everybody laugh—everyone but Larry. Without a word he had stood up, taken the record off, and put it back in its jacket.

"Oh, Larry, he didn't mean that," Mom had said quickly. "It's real pretty. Honest! But it's so long, and we got us a program coming on at seven. I'll listen to it some Saturday when I'm doing the ironing."

But that was six months ago, and the record had never been out of its jacket again.

That was the kind of family he had. It was as though he had been born into the wrong one—as though he had the genes and chromosomes of somebody else, and had been transported here among these morons. He had even wondered once if there had been a switch at the hospital, if two women had accidentally walked off with the wrong babies. His own parents, he was sure, were reading Proust and learning Russian and studying the molecular theory. They weren't watching a game show on TV or playing bingo on Thursday nights.

"Sometimes this happens," the school counselor had told him once, "and one kid in a family is way out front. Maybe that's what's happened to you. If so, just consider it a lucky break, Larry, and don't go around knocking them. They're the only family you've got."

That's right. For better or worse. He thought about that. If he had been born with three legs or water on the brain or a gross back deformity, would they have left him at the hospital and come home empty-handed? No, he knew they wouldn't. Mom was so kindhearted

she'd feed every stray animal that came around. She hated injustice, and when she listened to her favorite country singer belting out songs of mistreatment or misery, tears actually came to her eyes. "Don't make no difference who a person is, there's no excuse bein' mean to 'im," she always said.

And Dad? He didn't know a thing about Proust or Shakespeare or molecular theory, but he was a darn good mechanic, the shop foreman at Sears auto repair. He never missed a day of work if he could help it, he was honest with employees, and he detested shoddy work. People came from other towns, even, to have their cars repaired because they knew they could trust his workmanship.

Now, as Larry watched the snow pile up on the window ledge, he wondered what intelligence is worth if it's not tempered with kindness, what knowledge is worth if it's used to humiliate someone. His parents may not have the culture he craved, but they had instilled in him something else.

It was time for turning over a new leaf, and he began it that day. Just as the tension between them had come on slowly, the new relationship would have to build slowly too, one remark upon another.

That afternoon he repeated a compliment he'd heard at school about Sears being the best place to take your car. His father beamed.

"It's a nice feeling," Dad said. "You give your whole life to a job, you like to know it's appreciated, know what I mean?"

Yes, Larry knew what he meant.

He told his mother later that her apple cobbler was delicious. She liked to hear it, too.

"That was Grandma Baird's recipe," she said. "Been in the family all these years—ever' one of us sisters, we all use that recipe."

And so the weeks went by. Nothing big happened. There was no eye-opening discussion. Larry went ahead doing things that were important to him and talking to his counselor about colleges and preparing for his own life. But he didn't leave his books on the stand in the living room and he didn't try to talk above their heads. If he thought of something that might interest them, he tried it out at the dinner table —told them a little of something he'd learned. If they paid attention, he told them more and kept it simple. If they weren't interested, merely polite, he changed the subject and resisted the urge to be condescending.

It was easier than he'd thought. Respect, that was the answer. Now and then Bob made a remark about the Big Brain, but Larry ignored it. His father quit complaining because Larry stayed after school Wednesdays for an advanced chemistry course and Larry quit griping because his dad always left his grease-stained clothes at the bottom of the basement stairs for people to trip over. Slowly, in small ways, an attitude of kindness and tolerance was reinstated, something that had been missing for a long time.

And one Saturday, when Larry had slept late, he woke to the unmistakable sound of Mozart's fortieth coming from the kitchen, and he knew that Mom was ironing.

Change in the Wind

She knew when she awoke that things couldn't go on the way they had. Perhaps it was the gray sky, the same announcer's voice over the clock radio, the same bustle in the kitchen below. . . .

Mechanically Marlene climbed out of bed and groped to the bathroom, where she stepped on the scale. A half-pound more instead of less. She'd been dieting, supposedly, for six weeks, had lost three pounds and gained back two. The story of her life. It wasn't anything as serious as drugs or promiscuity or failing in school. It was the accumulation of small, everyday things that she felt she could tolerate no longer.

There were footsteps in the hall, and someone pounded on the door.

"C'mon, Mar, I got to brush my teeth! I'll miss the bus!"

"For heaven's sake, I just got in here!" Marlene's voice was shrill. She threw open the door with a scowl on her face, glaring at thirteen-year-old Rusty, who pushed by her and turned on the water in the sink.

Marlene went back to her room and sat down on the bed. If she'd gotten up sooner instead of listening to the radio for twenty minutes, she would have been out of the bathroom by the time Rusty needed it. Every morning the same hassles, the same problems, the same grayness, the same sameness . . . on and on and on. . . .

She looked up and caught her reflection in the mirror: blondish red hair, slightly plump face, medium shape—same expression, same Marlene.

She was quiet at breakfast. She always was, but this morning it was a different quiet, as if a small seed had been planted the moment she saw herself in the mirror.

"Want the comics?" her father asked, leafing through the newspaper.

"No. Not this morning," Marlene answered, absorbed in the feeling that something was going to happen. Something just had to.

"Don't forget to pick up your skirt at the cleaners," her mother called as Marlene left for school. But Marlene scarcely heard.

Down the steps, across the wet sidewalk. It was the first day of the month, she remembered suddenly. A new beginning, maybe?

She remembered another first of the month—January first, New Year's Day. The youth group at church had held a watch service instead of a party, and as the first few minutes of the new year crept in upon them, they all silently dedicated themselves again to God.

It had been such a beautiful moment, and Marlene had walked home in a swirl of snowflakes, singing carols with the others and feeling the joy of aliveness. How did it happen that she slipped so quickly back into the old routine, the old habits, the old way of behaving that made others dislike her at times? She even disliked herself.

Hadn't she always been a Christian? Hadn't she been raised in the church by Christian parents and patterned her life after the teachings of Christ? Shouldn't she be able to sail through each day in joy and anticipation, saying and doing the right thing at the right moment?

Instead, there was the constant bickering with Rusty, her fury at her mother's nagging, her chronic envy of one of the girls at school, her tendency to make remarks that really hurt. Sometimes it seemed as if she couldn't do even the simplest things—diet off a few pounds or arrange her time better on Saturdays. Each evening she prayed for guidance and support, and each morning the same trivial troubles faced her all over again. And yet, as she walked to school this morning in the gray dampness, something made her feel that perhaps there was a change in the wind.

She knew for sure that something was about to happen when she walked in the door at school and saw Jennifer Collins coming toward her down the corridor. In another ten seconds they would pass.

Jennifer had everything a girl could want—looks, clothes, money, even her own car—and to top it off, she was kind. People gravitated around her because she treated them well, and it had always seemed like just too much for Marlene to bear. Girls like Jennifer were supposed to be witches underneath—all the novels said so. Marlene watched her constantly, but she could discover no serious flaws, so she disliked her all the more. Whenever they passed in the hall, Marlene either looked the other way or said a tight, "Hi." The same, reluctant greeting. . . .

Suddenly, on this morning as Jennifer approached, Marlene knew the only way to say something different was to say something different. Just open her mouth and do it. With a tremendous effort she forced her lips into a smile and said, actually said, "Hi, Jennifer. I like your boots. They go well with that dress."

Jennifer gave her a surprised smile. "Why, thanks, Marlene."

A few seconds at the most, and it was over, yet Marlene felt exhilarated, as if she'd climbed Mt. Everest. It was a small battle, but she had won. She wasn't fighting Jennifer, she was fighting herself.

There was something about Jennifer's warm smile that encouraged her. It felt good saying something friendly, but could she keep it up? Marlene didn't know. All she knew was that at the moment she had found the courage to say something generous to someone she envied.

Lunch time. Another battle. However strong she thought she was, Marlene knew that in reality she could be ruled by a single piece of blueberry pie or a glazed doughnut. She stood in line in the cafeteria, adding up the calories in a bowl of soup and a glass of iced tea. No, she couldn't do it. Her stomach would rumble all through Algebra II, and she'd stop off on the way home and load up with pizza. Her resolve was fading. She would go on forever being somewhat overweight, the same Marlene—cheeseburger, french fries, and milk.

As she reached the counter, her eyes caught the calendar on the wall—the first of the month, a new day. All right, she would order one less thing than usual. That much she could do.

"Cheeseburger and milk," she requested. She closed her eyes as she moved past the desserts and on to the cashier. She did it. Another battle won. A small one.

The way to change behavior is to change behavior. She smiled to herself as she sat down in algebra class and opened her notebook. You can't just wish that you could do something differently—you do it! Even if it's only a small step. So simple! Why hadn't it worked before?

She was feeling good as she walked home from school. Her step was brisk and her head high. She quickened her steps as she passed the Pizza Shack, and for one awful moment, almost turned and went back. But she kept walking.

"Did you remember to pick up your skirt at the cleaners?" asked her mother when she heard her come in. "I thought you said you'd do it on your way home and save yourself a trip!"

"So I'll take a little walk!" Marlene said impatiently. "Is that so awful?" She stopped, remembering. "Anything I can pick up for you on the way over?"

There was surprise in her mother's voice. "Well . . . a gallon of skim at Thompson's, maybe."

"Will do. See you later."

It wasn't so easy, however, with Rusty. After dinner, she had one of the worst fights with him she'd ever had.

"Good grief, what happened to my pastels?" she cried, going into the den, where her artist chalk was broken in pieces.

"They dropped," Rusty said uncomfortably, from back in the living room.

"What do you mean, *they* dropped! You dropped them!" Marlene shrieked. "Look at them! Every single stick is broken! And my sketches are scattered all over the place!"

"The wind must have blown them around," Rusty yelled, leaping out of his chair and going to the door of the den to see for himself. His foot landed on one of the sketches, leaving a big footprint on the face of a little girl.

In blind fury, Marlene grabbed his hair, her nails digging into his scalp. Rusty yelled and swung at her. Like two caged animals they tore at each other till Mr. Elliott's voice brought them to a sudden halt.

"Marlene, you're sixteen, not three! Aren't you kids ever going to grow up?"

Tears welled up in Marlene's eyes. "Look what he did!" she cried. "My whole portfolio is scattered around the room!"

"I didn't do it!" Rusty yelled again. "I might have dropped your chalk, but I didn't have anything to do with the papers!"

"Okay, Rusty, get your money and pay for the

chalk," Mr. Elliott said. "Then do you suppose I could have an hour's peace before I go to bed?"

Marlene lay face down on her bed. She had not only failed this one, she'd failed miserably. It seemed to negate all the other little successes of the day. A ridiculous, hair-pulling free-for-all! *I can't do it,* she wept. *God, I can't do it!* In the silence that followed, she almost expected to hear the roll of thunder and a voice from out of the clouds. Instead, Rusty's half-hesitant twang came from the doorway.

"Here's the buck seventy-five, Mar. Listen, I'm sorry about that footprint on your sketch."

Marlene reached for a tissue and sat up, avoiding Rusty's eyes. "That's okay," she mumbled. "It wasn't one of my better sketches."

Rusty noticed her red eyes and hung on, wanting to make up. "You may not play volleyball so good, but you sure can pull hair," he said finally.

Marlene had to smile. "Well that's the last time I'm going to do it. I may scratch or kick you in the shins, but I won't pull your hair."

"Hey, that's real great of you," said Rusty, and they both laughed.

Marlene sat at her desk, working on her history assignment. Her mind wandered, and she scribbled, "Joyful, yes—easy, no," in the margin. Maybe that's what being a Christian was all about. Whoever said it was easy? All this time she had supposed that Christianity would automatically make her say and feel and do the right thing, without any effort, any sign of a struggle. Now she knew she would be struggling all her life. Could she do it?

Yes, but not all at once. She could not change her feelings overnight, but she could change her behavior, even if only one small change each day. There would be days she would fail horribly, she knew. But never again would she let them serve as excuses for not trying.

Not This
Mother,
Not This Day

There was always gossip. Joyce set her Coke down and stared back at the two women who were glancing at her from the neighboring booth.

"Friends of yours, Mom?" she asked.

Mrs. Lerner stopped jabbing at her tuna salad and turned around. "Huh. With friends like those, a person doesn't need enemies. They work in girls' clothing on the third floor. Not even worth discussing."

"Then let's don't," Joyce said, smiling. It was pleasant meeting Mother downtown occasionally for lunch, and she didn't want anything to ruin it. Usually she was so busy with school activities, and Mom, as manager of sportswear at Maxwell's, was so involved with customers and salesmen that the two rarely had time to say more than "Good morning" each day at breakfast.

Some evenings Mrs. Lerner didn't get home until eleven or later, and Joyce would make herself a cheese sandwich and eat alone. Other evenings, if Joyce had play rehearsal or choir practice, it was she who

111

would be home late, and often Mom was in bed by the time she came in.

And so they filled their days and evenings to the brim and kept themselves so busy that they didn't have much time to think about the divorce which only last year had made them a two-member family.

It was amazing how little she really knew about her parents, Joyce mused as she finished her dessert. Incompatability covered a multitude of sins, and neither her mother nor her father—whom she saw only occasionally—would talk about the other, pretending, instead, that the person with whom they had shared seventeen years of their life didn't even exist. Both said they were sorry things hadn't worked out, and yet they both assured Joyce it was for the good of everybody. Now figure that one out.

"Thanks for the lunch," Joyce said, as they moved toward the cashier. "Tomorrow I'm taking you out— someplace really special."

"Now, dear, there's no need. . . ."

"Mother's Day, you know."

"Why, I'd completely forgotten."

They crossed at the corner, and Joyce left her mother on the second floor where a New York salesman was already waiting.

"Back to the old grind," Mrs. Lerner said, giving Joyce a quick kiss. "Defrost the hamburger when you get home and I'll whip up something Hungarian."

Joyce took the escalator back to first and went over to blouses. She knew exactly what she was going to buy Mother. She'd seen it when she came in, thought about it during lunch, and decided it was perfect—

a pale green blouse with delicate dacron pleats in front. It would look great with Mother's beige suit.

"I'll charge it," Joyce told the clerk, taking out her own credit card.

The clerk looked at the name and then at Joyce. "Oh, yes, I thought you looked familiar." She began writing up the purchase. "You're Edith Lerner's daughter, aren't you?"

"Yes."

"You have the same look about the eyes," the woman said.

Instantly Joyce bristled, but didn't know why. She was getting so wary of people that anyone who even mentioned Mom was suspect. Actually, the clerk seemed quite friendly.

"A present for your mother, I'll bet."

"Yes."

"She'll like it. It's lovely."

She had to quit letting herself be affected by gossip, Joyce decided. If not, she was no better than the tongue-waggers themselves. Still, it was hard when you sensed it so often—the whispers, stares, knowing smiles.

Cathy, Joyce's long-time friend, had been the first to say something. It wasn't malicious. Cathy simply said whatever came to mind.

"Boy!" she had said a few months earlier. "I guess it pays to move away after a divorce. If not, the gossip can kill you!"

"What gossip? About Mom?"

Cathy had looked surprised that she didn't know.

"Oh, the usual corny stuff. Running around. That kind of thing."

Joyce had laughed. "She doesn't have time. Mother works too hard for that."

"I know. People will say anything to drum up a little excitement, won't they?"

"I guess it's the hours she keeps and the little trips she has to take. It's all part of her job. A buyer has to spend a lot of time with salesmen. People are bound to talk."

At home, Joyce took the blouse and held it up against Mother's suit in the closet. Beautiful. Exactly Mother's taste. It took eighteen dollars of Joyce's hard-earned money, but she wanted Mom to have something really nice this year, not the hose and handkerchiefs that had characterized Mother's Day gifts in the past.

She folded it lovingly and covered it with tissue paper. Then after decorating the box carefully with gold ribbon, she put it into her dresser till the following day.

Mother surprised her by coming home early.

"Listen, darling, something's come up. I thought we could have the evening together, but a salesman's here with samples from the fall line. It's either tonight or tomorrow, and you said you had plans for Mother's Day. . . ."

"Don't worry about it," Joyce told her. "Cathy's coming over. We'll manage."

"Oh, I'm glad! I'd hate to have you eat alone. Invite

her for dinner, and I'll set it up for you on the patio. It's so warm tonight."

"Cathy would like that," Joyce said, helping slice onions for goulash. "What's the fall line like? Have you seen it yet?"

"Lots of buttons and pockets and stuff—nothing outstanding, but the jackets are nice." Mrs. Lerner bustled about the kitchen, happy to be making dinner for Joyce. Joyce liked seeing her this way, even though she seemed frenetic at times.

Mother was gone by the time Cathy arrived, but she'd left a gaily decorated table on the patio with a steaming casserole in the center. There was even a vase of azaleas.

"Joyce, this is elegant!" Cathy said. "Does she serve you like this every evening?"

Joyce laughed. "No. She was just sorry she couldn't eat with us. Business again."

Cathy sat down. "You'll never guess what happened today."

"What?"

"I got my driver's license."

"You didn't! Oh, Cathy, that's great!"

"Didn't you see me drive up? Dad said I could use the car tonight."

"Wonderful! Where shall we go?"

"Let's drive out to Tolman's for a sundae. We'll celebrate."

They left about nine, taking a tour of the town—the high school, tennis courts, park, church. Finally, at ten o'clock, they headed out into the country for the homemade ice cream that made Tolman's famous.

Cathy had just passed Briggs' crossing and turned into the parking lot when Joyce cried, "Hey, Cathy, it's Mom!" She rolled down her window and was about to call out to the man and woman crossing in front of them when something held her back. And suddenly, as she stared, she saw the man put his arm around her mother as they headed for the motel next door.

Joyce drew in her breath sharply, and for a moment or two she felt she couldn't breathe at all. Then her mind began to race and she said quickly, "This must be where the salesman's staying. Probably got scads of samples to show her." Even as she watched, however, the salesman unlocked room 28, and he and Joyce's mother went inside.

Cathy pulled jerkily into a parking place without answering, and Joyce kept up the steady chatter. "C'mon. I'm starved. Let's go into Tolman's."

For almost an hour they sat over their chocolate sundaes discussing trivial things about school, watching the motel from the window. The lights had gone out in number 28.

Suddenly Joyce could stand it no longer. She covered her face with her hands. "I've got to know, Cathy," she said. "I've got to know for sure."

Cathy toyed with her spoon. "You're not going over there, are you?"

"No. I'm going to call."

With shaking fingers she deposited a coin in the phone in the booth outside. She dialed the motel number, and when the desk clerk answered, she said, "Room 28, please."

"Hello." It was the voice of the salesman.

"Excuse me," Joyce said. "Did you ask for a television set in your room?"

"What? We've *got* a television set. We've gone to bed and don't wish to be disturbed. You've got the wrong room."

Joyce leaned her head against Cathy and began to sob. Now she knew. All the things people had said over the past six months were true. "I want to go home, Cathy," she said.

"Listen, Joyce, we're friends, and nothing can change that. Nothing at all. Do you understand?"

Joyce nodded. It helped, and yet it didn't.

Cathy let her off in front of the house. Like a mad woman, Joyce rushed inside. She flung open the drawer, yanked out her mother's present and—as if flinging at her mother every wisp of gossip she had ever heard —she hurled the gift across the room, crashed it against the wall, smashed it again and again against the dresser.

In moments, the box was dented and the ribbon frayed. Joyce sank exhausted on the rug, weighted down with the ache in her arms and the even heavier ache in her heart.

"Not *this* mother!" she wept. "Not *this* day—not in *this* house, there won't be a Mother's Day."

It was eleven before she got up and dressed for bed. She took the torn package and threw it into her closet, closing the door on the ribbon, and lay down.

Of course she had known. Way down in her secret self, she'd noticed the change in Mother after the divorce—the seductive clothes, the change in make-up. She'd noticed the gay, happy-go-lucky veneer that Mom put on for other people, hiding the despondent part of her which spent spare time in front of the TV, watching but not seeing. She'd noticed the dramatic shift in her working hours and assumed it had something to do with Mother's promotion at the department store. But not all.

It was after midnight when Mrs. Lerner came in. Joyce heard her stop outside her bedroom door and then go on into her own room.

Joyce slept fitfully. At three o'clock she had a wild impulse to rush into her mother's room and confront her. She dozed again, and at four she awoke and decided instead to slam the bedraggled gift down on the breakfast table the next morning and say, "That's the way I feel about *this* mother on *this* day!"

When she woke again at six-thirty, she got up, washed her face, and took the tattered package downstairs, placing it conspicuously on the table. Taking a bowl of cereal into the dining room, she passed the patio door and stopped. There were the flowered plates that Mom had put out especially for last night. There were the bright orange napkins and the vase of azaleas.

Tears welled up again as she thought of all the little ways Mom had tried to make her happy, to fill the void that Dad had left—how she'd encouraged her to try out for the senior play, helped her plan a sixteenth birthday party, made her friends welcome here so there wasn't an empty moment left for brooding. However wrong, she was trying to do the same for herself. In a desperate search for love, she was settling for something far less, and pretending it was what she wanted. What a horrible mistake.

Joyce turned and stared at the disheveled package on the kitchen table. All she was doing was adding another rejection to an already rejected woman. She grabbed it, ripped off the ribbon, and hurriedly got out new wrapping paper to redo it. As she folded the blouse again, she felt no anger, but instead a deep sympathy for her mother, and a touch of love—certainly not for what Mom was doing, but for what she had been once, and what she might yet become.

She wrapped the box again and stuck some of the azaleas from the patio under the ribbon. Eventually, when she could trust herself to be sympathetic and understanding, she would have to tell Mother that she had seen her at the motel and that she was deeply hurt and disappointed. If she didn't, the resentments would grow until they got out of control. But on this one special day, she was going to treat her mother with all the kindness she could muster. And she would try, as hard as she possibly could, whatever happened, not to withdraw any of her own love from the mother who needed it now so desperately.

The Smoke
of the Pit

He'd been there since four o'clock that morning—sitting on the hard pew of the little church—holding Mom close against his chest and listening to the wailing of the women, which alternated with bleak silence.

The telegram had arrived at the university at one o'clock, but he couldn't get a bus out of Morgantown till two-thirty. It hadn't mattered. Nothing more had happened since the explosion except more smoke from the pit and the recovery of two bodies near the main entry.

Dawn was beginning to break over the West Virginia hills, but the grime and dust from the smoldering mine seemed suspended in the air, hiding the red sunrise.

"If the men near the shaft couldn't make it, Ward, the others won't either," Mother said, pulling away from him for a moment, her red eyes swollen, unnatural. "Seth's already gone. I feel it."

"Feeling's nothing to do with fact," Ward told her, patting her shoulder. "We've been through it before,

120

and you felt it then too, but it didn't happen. Remember '66? Almost went and bought yourself a funeral dress, when up he came." He tried to make her laugh, but he couldn't. "How many times has it been, Ma, you and me waiting like this? Three? Four? We can do it again. Waiting's the worst part."

But that wasn't entirely true. Anger was the enemy. Sitting there seething with the fury he couldn't show was the worst.

By six o'clock cars began pulling up outside the church—the waiting station for all the mine disasters the town had ever known. Women from neighboring villages were bringing in pans of scrambled eggs and toast, orange drink and coffee. They spread the food on a table near the back and tried to persuade the grieving families to eat.

"Try a little something, Mrs. Jacobs," one woman said, spooning eggs onto a paper plate and placing it on Mother's lap. "Seth comes out of the pit and you won't even have the strength to hug 'im."

Mother mechanically put the fork in her mouth.

"I'm going out for a stretch," Ward said. "I'll eat something later."

The smell of the explosion was strong in the air. Like a giant chimney, the shaft of No. 17 continued to belch smoke. The cage house and man hoist were charred in a heap of twisted metal. Any man who had been working near the pit was obviously dead. Who knew how many men had survived in the labyrinth of tunnels, or where they would be found, if they were found? The fear that paralyzed even the strongest man was that their disaster signal might never be heard, and that the mine would be sealed to cut off the raging fires.

To relieve his tension, Ward strode rapidly up the road, arms swinging from his shoulders. Cars marked "Press" came swarming like vultures to pick up the morbid details and print them for all the world to see.

"Say, mister, you a relative of one of the miners?" a young reporter called.

Ward ignored him and pushed on. It couldn't go on like this. It couldn't. He couldn't go four years at the university waiting for the telegram saying there had been another explosion and Dad hadn't been found. He couldn't live this way, he couldn't study knowing that the possibility of disaster hung like a huge boulder above them all, ready to drop at any moment. If Dad was dead—well, there was nothing more to be done. In spite of everything, he had insisted on going back down into the pit to fill his lungs with the coal dust that would kill him if an accident didn't do it first.

But if he lived—if he came up alive from this disaster, probably worse than all the others—Ward was giving him an ultimatum. Either Dad retired from the mines and took a job somewhere else, or Ward was cutting himself off from the family—not maliciously, but for self-preservation. It wasn't fair to ask for Mom and him to live on the edge of catastrophe, wasn't fair that they should have to sit there in the church watching each other age under the strain, when there were other jobs around. If Dad went down again, after all this, there would be no more telegrams to Morgantown, no more letters about what the company would or wouldn't do, no more talk of the safety regulations which were never completely met. He would be no part of it again—not ever.

The news that continued to come in wasn't good. An hour later there was a second, smaller explosion, and smoke was coming now from the south portal, where it was hoped the men might have gone to escape.

Mrs. Jacob's sister arrived from Baltimore, and the two clasped each other and wept.

"I've got to walk, Mom," Ward said desperately. "I can't stay here."

She understood. "Go on, Ward. I know how it is."

He left quickly, heading back into the woods, away from the cameras and notebooks of the reporters.

The unbearable part was Dad's stupid pride, the fierce love/hate affair with the pit that had drawn him to it when he was only seventeen. "The hellhole of the earth," he had called it many times. And yet he went. And more than that, Ward suspected that he secretly hoped his son would follow. It was tradition. It was the way it had always been in the Jacobs' family, because where else could a man really prove he was a man?

"Big beast of a man," Ward breathed to himself, even as the guilt welled up in him for daring to think it. "Clawing his way through the earth." Why should he and Mom have to suffer like this, over and over again, just so he could prove himself? How much proof did it take to know that a man was an idiot for going down into the dark, dangerous hole where men had been sealed forever?

"Ward!" An old man, crippled in one leg, stood holding on to the fence, looking in the direction of the smoke. "I heard the whistle go off early this morning. Any word on your father yet?"

"Not yet."

The man reached out and touched his arm in a gesture of sympathy. "The Lord be with 'im," he said. "There's not another man like Seth in these mountains. Not a one."

Ward waited awkwardly while the old man wiped a sleeve across his forehead and blinked once or twice. "Back in the sixties, when I was too old to be workin' the mines anymore but was doin' it anyway, he saved my life. He ever tell you that?"

Ward shook his head.

"It was the blast in the north end, where Perry Hawks got his arm blown off. The tunnel was full of fire and we were runnin' like the devil hisself was touchin' our heels. I slipped and broke my ankle. Your pa was clear to the main entry before he realized I wasn't behind him no more. Back he come, through the smoke, and got me." He blinked again. " 'Seth,' I says, 'you oughtn't to risk it, you know—the family you got.' 'Wouldn't be no respect from them if I'd left you here,' he says, and carried me all the way to the shaft. That was the way he was."

Ward wanted to get away. He plunged even higher up the hollow, away from the trail. But he'd forgotten the Benning family. Martha Benning was picking blackberries when he suddenly came upon her. She was working feverishly in an effort to keep her mind off the catastrophe below.

"It's a pie I'm bakin' for your mother, Ward," she said. "Just come up from the church and heard the news about the south portal." She began to weep. "Remember that spell when the coal was comin' slow and the men were workin' a day or two every three weeks? It was your dad who came bringin' bread and tinned meat—anything extra he could spare, and you hardly had enough for your own table. I always remembered that. I always said that if the Jacobses were wantin', I'd see to it myself. And now . . . now Seth'll likely not even taste the pie. . . ."

"There's no word yet, one way or the other," Ward said. "Always hope until they seal the mine—it's what Pa always said."

"Yes, that's true." She dabbed at her eyes. "I shouldn't be talkin' this way. Many's the time he's spoke comfortin' to me when my man was trapped down there. Sure it'll be okay. Sure it will."

He made certain this time that there weren't any people around. He climbed up the ridge as far as he could go and sat overlooking the mine—the black, smoking hole that had claimed a fourth of the men in the town. For almost an hour he sat there, wrestling with the fury. Men had to be mad, didn't they, to go into such a place? Was it fair to the families—this flirting with danger? As long as even one other job was available, wasn't it stubbornness that drove the men to the mine?

He realized suddenly how long he'd been away and knew he had to get back to his mother. Perhaps there would be some news by now. Perhaps they had found Seth's body and the long wait would be over.

With pounding heart, he got up and started rapidly back down the ridge. Did he really want it to happen?

Even before he reached the church, he knew there was news of some kind, for men were running and cars were streaming up the road from Clarksburg.

"Mom," he said, falling onto the pew beside his mother. "Any word?"

"Oh, Ward, I'm afraid to hope, but they've heard a tapping on an air vent in the west field. They think some of the men might be waiting there for rescue. They're setting up the rig and bucket now."

Ward sprang from the pew and followed the running men to the west field. It had happened before. It wasn't impossible. Sometimes a few men managed to hole up near an air vent, where the rush of air down the pipe kept the flames and smoke back long enough for a rescue bucket to be lowered.

Why did it take so long to remove the cap on the vent? Ward clutched at his head in anguish as he crouched on the ground and waited. Why did it take so long to get the hoist into position, to drop the cable with the scoop bucket attached?

Someone crouched beside him. "I'm hopin' it's Seth," said the voice of one of the other miners. "But if it ain't . . . I thought you'd like to know what your pa was sayin' about you. Just last week him and me was talkin' 'bout kids, and he told me how you were goin' to college. 'I'm makin' it my way and Ward's makin' it his,' he said. 'And I'm right proud of the boy.'"

Ward closed his eyes. "Thanks," he said. "I'd . . . I'd like to remember that."

126

Slowly the bucket went down and all was quiet except the creak of the hoist. Slowly, much too slowly, it returned with a grime-covered miner inside, and a cheer went up. The man stumbled out—a miner from up the hollow. White tear marks were etched in the coal black on his cheeks.

"How many more?" the people shouted. "Who's down there? How many?"

"There's eight of us," the man gasped, gulping down the water which was thrust in his hand. "Don't know them all for sure, but there's Robbie Sanders and Seth Jacobs. . . ."

Ward turned his face away as the heaviness in his heart lifted. He waited for the familiar resurgence of anger. A blinding flash of fury always came over him just after he found out his father was safe. When the worry was gone, the anger doubled.

But this time it didn't happen. This time he had spent the bitterness that festered inside. Instead, he felt a strange mixture of relief and gratitude, and suddenly he wanted to tell his father so. If Dad could go through hell down there, then he'd do it up here for as long as Dad held out. If Dad needed the mine, the miners needed Dad. This was his place, where he could give of himself, and nowhere else was he needed more.